Redesigning Collegiate Leadership

Redesigning Collegiate Leadership

Teams and Teamwork in Higher Education

Estela Mara Bensimon

Anna Neumann

THE JOHNS HOPKINS UNIVERSITY PRESS

BALTIMORE AND LONDON

© 1993 The Johns Hopkins University Press
All rights reserved
Printed in the United States of America on acid-free paper

The Johns Hopkins University Press
2715 North Charles Street
Baltimore, Maryland 21218-4319
The Johns Hopkins Press Ltd., London

Library of Congress Cataloging-in-Publication Data

Bensimon, Estela Mara.
  Redesigning collegiate leadership : teams and teamwork in higher
education / Estela Mara Bensimon and Anna Neumann.
    p.   cm.
  Includes bibliographical references and index.
  ISBN 0-8018-4561-0
  1. Educational leadership—United States.   2. Education, Higher—
United States—Administration.   3. Work groups—United States.
I. Neumann, Anna.   II. Title.
LB2341.B4745   1993
378.1'07—dc20   92-29728

A catalog record for this book is available
from the British Library.

Contents

Acknowledgments

We are deeply indebted to the presidents and vice presidents of the fifteen institutions who gave us many hours of their very busy days for interviews. Without their cooperation and their willingness to be open about what often proved to be sensitive topics of conversation, this project would not have been possible. We are also very grateful to our institutional contact persons for their assistance in scheduling our interviews and coordinating our visits. Because we promised our research participants anonymity we cannot acknowledge them by name here, nor can we name the institutions that so graciously received us. Even so, we wish to tell each and every one of them once more how very grateful we are for their participation.

Our understanding of leadership teams has also been enhanced by the generous assistance of several college presidents who participated in a focused dialogue held at the 1989 annual meeting of the Council for Independent Colleges: Louis J. Agnese, Jr. (Incarnate Word College), Rose Marie Beston (Nazareth College of Rochester), Thomas Boyd (Lambuth College), JoAnne Boyle (Seton Hill College), Michae Byron (College of Saint Teresa), John Burd (Brenau College), Richard I. Ferrin (Maryville College), Harold Kolenbrander (Mount Union College), Gretchen Kreuter (Rockford College), Daniel M. Lambert (Baker University), Joseph L. Lapp (Eastern Mennonite College), Dorothy I. MacConkey (Davis & Elkins College), Thomas K. Meier (Elmira College), Russell L. Nichols (Hanover College), John F. Noonan (Bloomfield College), Peter O'Connor (Aquinas College), William Pickett (Saint John Fisher College), George Poolaw (Flaming Rainbow University), William Robinson (Manchester College), Edward J. Rogalski (Saint Ambrose University), Samuel W. Speck, Jr. (Muskingum College), Sr. Francis Marie Thrailkill (College of Mount Saint Joseph), and Sr. Margaret Wick, O.S.F. (Briar Cliff College). Rusty Garth of the CIC, in particular, was most helpful in coordinating this session.

We wish to extend our deep gratitude to Mary Ann Sagaria and an anonymous reviewer for insightful comments that strengthened the content, form, and style of this book, and to Jacqueline Wehmueller, our editor at the Johns Hopkins University Press, for her attention, encouragement, and assistance in every way. We also thank the following individuals for thoughtful reviews of an early draft; their suggestions took

us a long way forward: Jean Armstrong, Robert Birnbaum, Shirley Cha-
ter, Kent Farnsworth, Richard F. Gross, Judith Dozier Hackman, Peggy
Heim, Joe Kauffman, Ted Marchese, Judith Block McLaughlin, Kathryn
Moore, Barbara Guthrie-Morse, Maria Perez, and Piedad Robertson.

We owe special thanks to three people who consistently offered us
outstanding research support. Kelly Ward, a graduate student at Penn
State's Center for the Study of Higher Education, and Jill Glickman, a
former graduate student at Teachers College, Columbia University, served
as research assistants on this project. Nancy Gearhart served as secretary
to the project. We are most grateful to Kelly for coordinating the work
of the review panels, and to Jill for assisting in project management and
particularly for preparing an early bibliography and resource library.

We also want to recognize Eleanor Fujita, a former doctoral student
at Teachers College, for her assistance in multiple ways throughout our
years in New York. Kevin Williams, also a former student at Teachers
College, conducted numerous library searches for us during the earliest
phases of the project. Kathryn M. McManus, who served as Teachers
College grants and contracts officer, was also especially helpful in organizing the business side of the project.

Over the years Peggy Heim and TIAA-CREF have been extremely
supportive of our work. Their encouragement and assistance with the
myriad details of this project are greatly appreciated.

Lastly, we wish to express our thanks to the Lilly Endowment for its
generous support of this study and to Ralph Lundgren, who served as
program officer for this project.

Bensimon and Neumann directed the study reported in this book jointly.
Each made an equal, although different, contribution to the book, and
the sequence of their names on the title page reflects only alphabetical
ordering.

Introduction

What is your image of good leadership? If you are like most people, you think of leadership as a rare and special talent, power, or expertise that only a few "chosen" individuals are lucky enough to possess. Although the study of leadership has traditionally focused on such special individuals—on their traits, behaviors, skills, or influence tactics—there is now considerable interest in looking at leadership not as a "one-person act" but as a collaborative endeavor. We are beginning to think of leadership not in terms of single individuals but in terms of *teams*. In particular, we see a growing interest in the dynamics of interactive leadership at the executive level in a variety of organizations, be they corporations, public agencies, or colleges and universities. We see the theme of collective and interactive leadership throughout the professional literature: We hear references to "the team as hero" (Reich 1987); we hear about the strengths of "integrative leadership" (Kanter 1983); and we attend to slogans like "Forget charisma, focus on teamwork" (Cox 1989).

The growing interest in team-oriented leadership has also provoked serious debate. Advocates of the collaborative perspective contend that team-oriented leadership makes it easier for organizations to adapt to technologically complex and information-rich environments (Zuboff 1988, Kanter 1983, Cleveland 1985). The central premise of the collaborative view is that learning is the most important activity of modern-day organizations. Kanter (1983) maintains that collaborative modes of management stimulate the search for solutions "beyond what the organization already 'knows' (or, to be more accurate, beyond what its leaders think they know)" (p. 29). Similarly, Zuboff (1988) writes that in the "age of the smart machine" the increased flow of information demands "a more team-centered, problem-solving orientation" (p. 360) so that organizations are in a position to "maximize [their] own ability to learn and explore the implications of that learning" (p. 398). In short, advocates believe that a team-centered managerial approach enhances the capacity of organizations to master new knowledge and to use it effectively to improve innovation, problem solving, and productivity.

Dissenters argue that the collaborative perspective is incompatible with the cultural values of North American society. They also maintain that a team orientation is inconsistent with characteristics most likely to elicit superior leadership. The crux of the dissenters' view is that North

American entrepreneurship is made possible by individualism (Fallows 1989); leaders (as opposed to managers) are the product of experiences that imbue them with a sense of separateness or apartness from those around them (Zaleznick 1989).

The individualist and the collectivist camps have debated mostly through research or other forms of discourse focusing on corporate organizations and through comparative international studies of organizations. For the most part, they have not yet addressed the leadership of academic organizations. Although college presidents and other campus leaders often espouse a teamwork ideology, what leadership teams offer academic organizations specifically is not clear. Most often, their usefulness is taken for granted and thus left unexamined.

The Study of Leadership Teams

Our knowledge of leadership teams is based primarily on a study that we collaboratively planned and implemented. During the course of the study, we twice visited fifteen institutions located throughout the United States, first in 1986–87 and again in 1988–89. During our second visits we conducted individual interviews with the presidents and up to four members of their leadership teams about the nature of the teams' organization, functions, and internal dynamics (a copy of the interview protocol is provided in Appendix A). In selecting interviewees we asked the presidents to identify up to four individuals whom they considered to be members of their leadership teams. For the most part, the presidents named the chief officers of typical college and university divisions—academic affairs, finance and administration, student affairs, and external affairs or development. We interviewed a total of seventy individuals on a one-to-one basis, spending approximately three hours with each president and an hour and a half with each of the other team members (many of whom carried the title of vice president, although others were deans, directors, executive assistants, and so forth). Additionally, because we were collecting data as part of a larger study (the Institutional Leadership Project of the National Center for Postsecondary Governance and Finance), we also conducted interviews with faculty and trustees. From these multiple views we were able to construct comprehensive images of leadership processes in the sample institutions. In addition to learning how the presidents and the persons whom they had designated worked together as a team, we collected data on how faculty perceive their administrative leaders, including their president, individual team members (e.g., vice presidents), and the leadership team collectively. Our data base included transcripts of the seventy personal interviews as well as comprehensive case studies for each of the fifteen institutions.

Although we spoke at great length with the presidents and members of their leadership teams, we did not observe them at work as teams. All of the data we present are derived exclusively from our interviews.

The fifteen institutions involved in the study are diverse. Four are research universities, four public comprehensive four-year colleges, four independent colleges, and three community colleges. Nine of the institutions are public and six are private. The sample is also diverse in terms of program emphasis and location, including, for example, a mixture of urban, suburban, and rural settings. Of the fifteen presidents, four are women. Eleven presidents were relative newcomers to their position (from one to five years in office); the remaining four had been in office for a minimum of seven years. In keeping with our promise of confidentiality, we use pseudonyms to mask institutional and individual identities, and we refer to all institutions as colleges, regardless of their real type. We also use generic rather than institutionally specific titles to designate roles, governance bodies, college events, and so forth. Readers desiring additional information on the study design, methods of data analysis and interpretation, and linkages to the long tradition of social psychological research on groups are urged to consult the formal reports resulting from this study (Bensimon 1991b, Neumann 1991c).

The intent of the study was to explore models of teamwork in higher education, taking into account the leadership orientations of presidents and their executive officers. Our interest was to examine how presidents and their designated team members work together; how team members perceive the quality of their working relationships; how presidents select, shape, and maintain particularly effective teams; and how teams address conflict and diversity of orientation among team members. Our conclusions are based on interview data collected at the fifteen participating institutions and also on the published research of others and our own experiences as participants in a variety of groups.

We hope that this book will be valuable to college leaders concerned with building effective leadership teams and promoting teamwork. The ideas set forth in this book may prove useful to vice-presidents, deans, department chairs, trustees, and other individuals who are part of teams, in addition to presidents. In chapters 1 and 2 we introduce the concept of the "leadership team" (or as we refer to it in our study, the "presidential team" or the "top administrative team"). Following a discussion of the advantages and disadvantages of teamwork (chapter 1), we contrast the conventional view of leadership as a "one-person act" to the thesis of this book—that leadership is a shared, interactive, culturally framed activity (chapter 2). In chapters 3, 4, and 5, we explore in greater detail how a team works when we think of it in cultural terms, including what leaders may hope to derive from team functioning (chapter 3), how team members think together (chapter 4), and how teams that work like complex social brains are designed (chapter 5). In these chapters we use a variety of case examples drawn from our study to make the point that what teams and their members do, and especially how they think, define the difference between "real" teamwork, on the one hand, and teamwork that we deem "illusory," on the other. Chapters 6, 7, and 8 are devoted to issues of team building, including how to develop teams that are inclusive (chapter 6) and responsive to complex campus changes (chapter 7). We conclude with principles of good teamwork and recommendations for team building (chapter 8). While the book speaks strongly to college and university presidents, it should also be of interest and use to other campus leaders who want to understand better their own (and their teammates') potential for contribution to a leadership team.

In an extensive review of leadership development programs, Sharon McDade (1987) indicates that at the present time, college and university presidents and other administrators have few training opportunities (other than "on the job") for learning about the workings of leadership teams and about strategies for building effective teams. In this book we give attention to what leaders can do to strengthen their skills in working with people. Thus we focus on defining the nature of administrative communication, the importance of interdependence, the necessary precursors of collaboration, and a number of related topics. We hope that our emphasis on what it takes for people to work together comfortably and productively will help to bring some balance to the attention that professional development programs are currently giving to more instrumental and managerial aspects of individual and team leadership (e.g., budgeting, formal organization, bureaucratic processes).

What Is a Team?

Although all the presidents participating in this study informed us that they had teams (and easily named the people we should interview), we learned very early in our research that the word *team* (like the word *leadership*) means many different things to different people. Not only do teams differ in the quality of their work (some are better organized, more efficient, and so forth, than others), but also in their style and in their group "personality." What this means, in part, is that the experience of being a team member can vary drastically from team to team. Here are two examples from our study:

Member of Team A: On a scale of 1 to 10 I would rate our team a solid 8. We view ourselves as sharing in a common enterprise. We don't see ourselves as working in isolation; it is an attitude about the institution. The team is very good for top-level decision making. For example, earlier this year I wanted to argue for the development of a new academic program. In the past, I would have convinced the president, but now under the new president, I have to justify the new program in the senior staff meeting. I have to convince all my colleagues that this is important enough so that they will give up resources for it. Working like this is an excellent way of arriving at institutional priorities. Someone might argue that it would be easier for me to make the decision alone, but the collective way is good for me because it means I have the full support of my colleagues. In the long run it makes my job easier.

Member of Team B: If I had to assess our team right now I would say that it is around a "D." We all work to support the president but not the team. We have not met in two months. In fact, we rarely have meetings of the whole team. We mostly just talk to each other individually. Things were not always this way. We disbanded our regular meetings about six months ago because there have been tussles over turf and over the budget. A lot comes up in my area that I need to inform people about or that I need to get reactions to, and it is harder to carry out that kind of interaction one to one. I would prefer meeting as a group.

Some teams work in very "teamlike" ways. Others seem remarkably unteamlike. In short, a "team" is not always a team. One of our purposes has been to examine such differences in how teams work and also to consider whether certain forms of teamwork are better—for the team and for the institution—than others.

In writing this book, we chose to show (rather than to tell) what good and not-so-good teamwork looks and feels like. To do this, we present extensive illustrations of life in leadership teams, including what presidents (and others) do to improve or hinder teamwork and what their inaction yields. Unlike traditional books on administrative management and leadership, we prescribe very little. Moreover, we do not provide the reader with the conventional (and all-too-simplified) lists of team dos and don'ts. Instead, we describe the patterns that we saw across our sample institutions, and we present the voices of multiple interviewees as they portray everyday life in presidential leadership teams.

We chose this more descriptive style deliberately, knowing that the market has a surfeit of how-to manuals, but mostly because we wanted to provide lifelike examples that our readers could identify with. The various images of team life that appear throughout this book should be familiar, particularly to readers who sit on presidential teams. We expect that our readers, on hearing other people describe their teams, will experience instant recognition, that they will mentally exclaim: "That is exactly what goes on in our group."

Our intent in describing the "doing" and "thinking" of teams, their coming together and coming apart, the feelings of connectedness and alienation that they engender, is to freeze the stream of team activity and to give readers an opportunity to examine, from the outside, phenomena that cross their own lives. Thus we view this book as an opportunity for reflection. We hope that in thinking about the experiences of other people in other teams our readers will gain insight into those aspects of their own "team life" that they should actively preserve and affirm, and those that they should change. And we hope that they will act accordingly.

A caveat: We want to emphasize that in using the term "team," we do not mean a group of people working harmoniously in pursuit of manager-determined goals and in machinelike form. On the contrary, we believe that a group that is free of conflict, that takes its cues only from the manager "in charge," and that emphasizes mechanical efficiency over an often simultaneous human clumsiness and creativity is unlikely to function as a team that leads, acts, and thinks together.

Why Write about Collaborative Leadership?

Our interest in teamwork dates back to 1986, when the two of us joined a research project on institutional leadership that was part of the former National Center for Postsecondary Governance and Finance. That year we traveled to twenty-eight institutions to interview presidents, vice presidents, faculty, and trustees in a massive effort to examine how college leaders interact and communicate with one another, how they assess their own and each others' effectiveness, how they develop their understandings of their campuses, and how they establish goals and transmit values.

On returning from our first-year visits we were intrigued with the idea of leadership as interactive, collaborative, and shared. It became increasingly difficult for us to think in terms of individual leaders without referring, at the same time, to their interactions (intended or not) with those around them. As we wrote our first conference papers and articles, mostly on presidential leadership, our interest in the balance and tension between individual and collective leadership grew.

Our interest in teamwork was also influenced by other sources—for example, by our observations of people working together in various committees, special project task forces, and research teams outside the study itself. In addition, the two of us have worked together as a team since 1986, experiencing the highs and lows that are bound to come when two very different people enter into a collaborative relationship. Through our own doing and thinking together, and through our friendship, we have gained special sensitivity to the kind of personal work required to keep a team together. Consequently, our work on teams is very much oriented by our personal experiences as well as by our beliefs about the meaning of good leadership. We have stated the beliefs that guide our work on leadership extensively elsewhere (see, for example, Neumann & Bensimon 1990). Some main points of those beliefs are:

- Organizational agendas and events do not arise solely from the president (or for that matter, from any solo leader). Rather, people working in interactive groups create and negotiate their realities over time.
- Despite the centrality of the interactive group (rather than the solo leader), a college president, as the team's first leader (and as its builder), has a unique opportunity to bring personal understandings and interpretations to bear on how the team members understand and feel about their shared reality. Other administrators in team-initiating roles hold exactly the same power in developing *their* teams.
- Regular team members (e.g., the vice presidents on the presidential team) do not serve purely as advisors, staff, or assistants to the person who initiated the team (e.g., the president). We have found, for example, that when presidents step out of public view they rarely do their homework alone. They are often joined by team colleagues—vice presidents, executive assistants, and others—who contribute as much, if not more, to institutional leadership as the president. It is high time that the myth of solo leadership, as applied to the presidency and to other leadership roles, be shattered. The presidency is lodged not in one person but in a team.
- Leadership is the shared construction of meaning (Berger & Luckmann 1966). Leadership requires skill in the creation of meaning that is authentic to oneself and to one's community. It also requires the uncovering of meaning that is already embedded in others' minds, helping them to see what they already know, believe, and value, and encouraging *them* to make new meaning. In this way, leadership generates leadership.

Redesigning Collegiate Leadership

1

Leadership by Teams: The Need, the Promise, and the Reality

Chief executive officers in industry, government, and education are operating in an increasingly complex and uncertain world. Rapid changes in technology, information, the labor force, and the economy will require future managers to exercise leadership in an increasingly turbulent environment (Morgan 1988). This will not be easy because rapidly changing environments are hard to see, hard to analyze, and hard to understand. The human mind is more attuned to stability than to flux: we are far more comfortable when we know what we'll get than when our expectations are muddled.

Writers who specialize in the subject of social change and how the human mind reacts to it remind us that human cognition is limited: that is, any one of us can sense and comprehend only so much. However, they also remind us that each of us is different. We differ not only in our viewpoints, values, and thinking modes but also in our limitations. Thus, what one person lacks another may possess, and what that person misses yet another may have. If only we could combine the minds of several people into one . . . Even then we might not gain full understanding of the turbulent, complex reality before us, but we would certainly cover more ground than we can cover working alone.

It is this wish for compounded vision and compounded talents—several individually talented minds rolled into one—that drives writers and researchers to project that, in a turbulent future, the ideal leader will not be a super solo hero who makes all the right decisions and tells others how to carry them out. Rather, the ideal leader will be someone who knows how to find and bring together diverse minds—minds that reflect variety in their points of view, in their thinking processes, and in their question-asking and problem-solving strategies; minds that differ in their unique capacities as well as in their unique limitations. The ideal manager of the future will be less an "expert" at some task than an orchestrator of multiple complex tasks. She or he will be able to pull a group of thinkers together and to facilitate their collective "mindwork." Moreover, as the world grows more complex—that is, as we come to appreciate its growing complexity—it is likely that we will stop thinking of leadership as the property or quality of just one person. We will begin to think of it in its collective form: leadership as occurring among and through a group of people who think and act together.

We would go so far as to say that even today, the best managers and leaders are not solo artists, even though the world imposes this view upon them. When these leaders shut their office doors to the public eye, they do not pore over their agendas alone and in silence. Rather, they are likely to talk, ask, ponder, and argue with a small group of co-thinkers who give as much of themselves to the issues at hand as the managers whom the public deems to be "in charge."

As a society we hold fast to the myth of one-person leadership. Our organizational structures reinforce it. In higher education, the relative absence of financial "hard times" in previous decades (i.e., the growth years) also served to reinforce the myth of solo leadership. It is only as resources have become scarcer and survival tougher that the truth of how leadership really happens has started to show through the cracks in organizational life. If, as many writers tell us, teams are the thing of the future, this is less because they represent something new than because they represent something that has already been in place for a long time. We have simply not brought the idea of leadership as a team—rather than as one person—to light.

The view of the manager as a team builder rather than as a heroic organizational captain is not new. However, even today there is a discrepancy between what our profession knows intuitively about the importance of teams and what our professional literature professes about the importance of leadership by individuals: Although the ability to develop a cohesive team has long been viewed as a characteristic of effective leadership, writers and researchers still emphasize the attributes and behaviors of individual leaders (e.g., what it takes to be a good college president) rather than *the overarching dynamics of a number of people in interaction with each other* (e.g., how college presidents and key members of their cabinets work together).

Despite higher education's long tradition of "shared collegial leadership" (Goodman 1962, Millett 1962), and despite contemporary calls for college executives to work together (Gardiner 1988, Guskin & Bassis 1985, Walker 1979), our professional literature tells us very little about how administrators and others build leadership teams, or about the specific leadership orientations of such teams. For example, we do not have a clear picture as to whether such teams are diverse or uniform in their composite leadership orientations, whether presidents, deans, or others who initiate teams select team members who are similar to or different from themselves, or whether certain kinds of team combinations are more effective than others. We do not even know who typically sits on prominent institutional teams (the president's or dean's leadership group), how team members view and relate to each other, and how they work together—or fail to do so.

In an incisive commentary, Eisenstat and Cohen (1990) explain why and how leadership, viewed as a team effort, is more effective than leadership defined as an individual endeavor. According to them:

A team's decisions are more apt to represent the wide range of interests present in any organization than would those of an individual leader acting alone.

There is a possibility for more creative organizational solutions from a group of individuals with different skills, perspectives, and information than there would be from any individual leader.

Team members, as well as organizational constituencies they represent, should better understand and be more apt to support organizational decisions that they have played a role in shaping.

Communication among top managers should be more efficient when they work as a team because they meet together regularly.

The job of managing an organization is simply too vast to be accomplished by any one individual leader; a team can spread the burden and ensure that important tasks receive adequate attention.

Serving in a top management group can provide valuable developmental experiences for members. (Pp. 78–79)

In sum, according to Eisenstat and Cohen, team-based leadership is apt to be more cognizant, alert, understanding, competent, talented, acceptable, efficient, equitable, and supportive than leadership by just one person.

But how do we know this? Would it not be more straightforward and more effective to rely on just one person to provide direction to a host of doers? Why clutter up leadership? In a study comparing the leadership strategies of successful and unsuccessful managers, John Gabarro (1987), in concurrence with Eisenstat and Cohen, found that the managers who succeeded in establishing records of success early in their jobs tended to rely on cohesive management teams, while managers with less spectacular records did not. In brief, Gabarro's study equates managerial success with team-based leadership and failure with a solo managerial act. Gabarro also found that unsuccessful managers tended *not* to work directly with their staffs in a group format but rather to deal with individual staff members separately or through formal, distanced means of communication. They also tended to avoid addressing preexisting conflicts among team members—trouble spots that can fester and grow over time. Gabarro concluded that the failure to form cohesive executive teams may be related to the presence of administrative leaders who are overly hierarchical, formal, and task oriented. Such administrators are likely to feel uncomfortable in the often chaotic atmosphere of groups and in sessions that are rife with human emotion.

Studies like these suggest that managers who can build cohesive teams hold an important key to managerial success. However, we urge caution with regard to this conclusion: It is conceivable that the presence of a cohesive team may be but a *sign* of success that has been caused by *other* organizational factors—and not by the team as such. Or it may be that the team is just one of a host of leadership and organizational factors that lead to success. We examine such prospects in more detail in chapter 5. In the meantime, one point is clear: a good team—as cause, as effect, or as signal—is part and parcel of good leadership. Therefore, in exploring how teams work, we are likely to be exposed to at least some of the tenets of good leadership.

Gabarro's study suggests that the manager's approach to team building and leadership generally is at least as important as whether or not a team is in place at all. As we will repeat later, having a good team builder is at least as important as having a good team.

The Advantages—That Is, the Promises— of Teamwork

Based on our research, our analyses of others' research, and our professional experiences and observations, we have identified several advantages of teamwork that contribute to good leadership. First, however, we caution our readers that because teamwork and team building are complex endeavors, it is important not to think of teams in terms of equations, rational principles of operation, or straightforward prescriptions. There is no equation for teamwork or for leadership generally. Good teamwork depends, not only on the individuals who compose the team, but also on innumerable institutional factors such as financial health, faculty and staff morale, the president's leadership orientation, design of governance, and so forth. But despite the contingencies and complexities, teams nonetheless reflect distinct advantages over solo leadership. Some examples follow.

Teamwork Can Mean Creative Problem Solving among Diversely Oriented Minds

Recent studies show that groups that respond successfully to problematic or challenging circumstances are composed of members with a high degree of diversity in both experience and point of view. Including group members with diverse thinking styles should increase the likelihood that the group will examine similar as well as competing perspectives on a given problem (Goleman 1988).

To foster cognitive diversity within the team, leaders may need to reframe conventional views of group work. For example, rather than striving to achieve a consistent or unified point of view in the spirit of consensus building, persons who seek to build creative teams would do better to focus on their team's potential for different modes of thinking. As we will explain later, group-oriented leadership strives to bring out more than what the group's members have in common. It strives also to bring out the differences among people—individuals' unique beliefs and perspectives—and to capitalize on them for the good of the group. It avoids consensus and compromise forged at the cost of critical thinking. Unfortunately, managers all too often take the opposite tack, focusing on commonality rather than on differences or complementarity, often at great cost to persons in the group and to the group itself.

To assemble a diverse group of people who are capable of working with each other, group-oriented managers need to be able to assess individuals for their "cognitive fit" with the rest of the team, including their abilities to contribute to its work. What do we mean by a group-oriented manager? We have found that group-oriented managers usually prefer to work collaboratively rather than alone, and they are usually very supportive of their administrative colleagues and others on the team, even though outsiders may think of the others as subordinates. Within the team, the sense of subordination typically disappears. Even outside the team, these managers treat their colleagues with utmost respect, crediting them fully for their unique contributions to the leadership group. However, the most important attribute of group-oriented managers is that they are *learners* prepared to have their minds changed by others who may know more about a particular subject than they do (Cox 1991) and who often understand and analyze reality differently than they do.

These managers typically know how to use their teams to do much more than simply get things done, a topic that we will explore at greater length in chapter 3.

Teamwork Can Facilitate Cognitive Complexity

In our previous work on leadership we have associated effective presidential leadership in colleges and universities with cognitive complexity. Effective presidents typically view their institutions in multiple ways—as bureaucratic hierarchies, as human enterprises, as political arenas, and as cultural systems (Bensimon 1989; Bensimon, Neumann & Birnbaum 1989; Birnbaum 1988). We have also found that cognitively complex presidents typically deploy complex strategy in getting things done: at times they act linearly according to a model of rational bureaucracy; at other times they are more flexible and adaptable to supervening circumstances; and at still other times, they assume interpretive roles in giving shape and meaning to confusing events (Neumann 1989).

Our research, however, also shows that (*a*) very few presidents demonstrate the ability to view their institutions through multiple lenses but rather tend to think of them only in political terms or only in bureaucratic terms (Bensimon 1989) and (*b*) very few have a large repertoire of strategies for addressing changing circumstances (Neumann 1989). Simply put, cognitive complexity is a valuable but altogether rare quality among college and university presidents. From our studies and conversations with a variety of institutional leaders, we would venture to say that these patterns apply to persons in other leadership positions as well.

As long as we regard cognitive complexity as a characteristic of a single individual, we will continue to think of it as a rare phenomenon. It is hard to find truly complex individuals. However, if we consider cognitive complexity to be a *team* characteristic, then its presence in an organization becomes eminently more likely. It is likely that multiple minds joined together will be much more complex than one mind working alone, regardless of its capabilities.

There is a down side, however: cognitive complexity that is team based cannot be achieved without considerable work on the part of the team builder and other members of the team. In chapter 3 we describe how leaders can use their teams to maximize cognitive complexity, and in chapter 4 we explain how team members may contribute to the cognitive complexity of their teamwork. In chapter 5 we look more closely at life inside a cognitively complex team—including what it is like to work in one—and we consider the extent to which teams may affect institutional performance.

Teams Can Provide Peer Support

While teams can be important at all levels of college and university life, they are likely to be especially important to the president because, as the college's chief administrative officer, the president has no campus-based peer. This, of course, is not true for most other campus-based leadership roles; typically there are several, even many, vice presidents, deans, department chairs, and so forth. In higher education as we know it today, there is only one president per campus. The president's administrative team can provide the support, assistance, and reinforcement that would otherwise be missing from the president's campus-based professional life (White 1986, p. 30). While off-campus friends (e.g., presidents at other institutions) are important, they are no replacement for colleagues who share the same campus reality.

In *The Effective Administrator* (1979), Donald Walker, an experienced administrator and long-time college president, maintains that a team approach can be particularly valuable if members cultivate the attitude of being "physicians to one another," thus creating mutually supportive environments for the resolution of both institutionwide problems and local departmental or divisional problems (e.g., academic affairs). A president in our study voiced a similar view: "When you get to this level these are lonely jobs . . . and having peer colleagues is not insignificant. [I look to them to] give me advice. . . . When there is a crisis [I want] to be able to sit down and ask them what we should do." The creation of a team that is supportive of all its members despite their differences—in fact, that capitalizes on such differences—is most challenging. We discuss the challenges of building diverse, complex, and supportive teams in chapters 6 and 7.

Teams Can Increase Accountability

Some presidents feel that the forced (albeit internal) openness of a group approach may encourage people to take responsibility for their actions, including their mistakes. A number of the presidents in our study commented that the internal openness of a team approach helps ensure that assignments are carried out. Discussion within the team requires members to disclose whether or not they are making progress or having trouble with certain tasks. One president told us, "I use the minutes [of group meetings] as a check, for gentle goading." Another president explained that the openness of a group approach is useful because it "controls the power games far better than is otherwise possible" because if everyone has access to similar information, it is harder to leverage it for individual agendas.

While some presidents may rely on their teams to enforce strict individual accountability or to maintain control, we caution that casting accountability as control is likely to undermine the team's potential for creative problem solving and cognitive complexity. Viewed purely as units for enforcing accountability or for asserting control, teams are likely to restrain creative thinking rather than to facilitate it. Thus while enhanced accountability has its advantages, it can also be restrictive and harmful. The balance between an accountability that generates openness, on the one hand, and an accountability that restricts creative thinking, on the other hand, is something that should be watched and managed with care. In chapter 8 we discuss how team members might organize themselves to reflect, as a group, on how they practice leadership, individually and collaboratively—for example, how team members might explore and talk about the patterns of openness and restrictiveness within the team and how, together, they might adjust dysfunctional group habits.

The Disadvantages of Teamwork: Some Hard Realities

Our research, alongside several other studies, shows that teamwork does not always live up to its promises. The seeming strengths of teamwork occasionally become weaknesses that may undermine the very things—creative problem solving, cognitive complexity, and so on—that we would expect to accomplish. For example, we often think of effective teams as composed of individuals who want to participate actively in all aspects of the team's work. As Lynn Oppenheim shows, however, team members may lapse into wanting to direct the work of others on the team rather than participating with them equally (Goleman 1988). This kind of situation can bring the team to a standstill.

The configuration of people on the team also merits attention as a potential problem area. Robert Sternberg asserts that teams need to balance intelligence and social skills among their members. A team that is strong either in intelligence or affability alone is seriously disadvantaged (Goleman 1988). Our own analyses of how team members interact, and how college presidents use their teams, reiterate the need to balance a variety of related factors—including the forms of thinking (e.g., analyzing, interpreting, critiquing, etc.) in which team members typically engage (Neumann 1991c) and the range of functions that the team as a whole can fulfill (Bensimon 1991b). Our research suggests that teams whose members think in diverse (as opposed to similar) ways and function flexibly across a variety of task types (rather than focusing just on one) are likely to be associated with effective leadership. We continue this discussion in chapters 3, 4, and 5.

To balance our discussion of the promises and advantages of teams we present here a brief sampling of the disadvantages and difficulties that teams may simultaneously present:

Teams Can Become Isolated

In our study we observed some teams that were so cohesive that they had, in effect, turned in on themselves and lost touch with the rest of the institution. While these teams exhibited a very high degree of mutual support and functioned very smoothly as teams, they were also extraordinarily distant from their institution. Even though team members saw their group as functioning very effectively from within (that is, work got done effectively and with minimal conflict), faculty were extremely critical of them, accusing them of indifference to what the rest of the campus thought of their work. Such teams invested a great deal of time in developing a shared style of leadership. However, by virtue of developing a distinctive and cohesive *administrative subculture*, they separated from— and, in fact, became alienated from—the *faculty subculture.*

Rosabeth Moss Kanter (1983) defines this excessive garnering of team spirit as "suboptimization":

> A group can become *too much* [italics in original] in its own goals and activities and lose sight of the larger context in which it is operating. For example, the kinds of things that can help pull a group together—a retreat offsite to communicate better, a sense of specialness and unique purpose, private language and working arrangements—can also wall it off from everyone else. . . . This is what management theorists call "suboptimization": a group optimizing its own subgoals but losing sight of the larger goals to which they are supposedly contributing. (Pp. 267–68)

When a team loses sight of the larger institution, it ceases to be effective and risks its own demise. One of our study teams suffering from "suboptimization" was stripped of its powers soon after the arrival of a new president, who became aware of the team's "separateness" from the rest of the campus. Unfortunately, because this president was not a strong supporter of the teamwork ethic that had long guided leadership at this institution, he crushed the idea of teamwork altogether, establishing himself as the primary leadership authority, rather than trying to reestablish a balance between internal team cohesion on the one hand and team openness to the campus on the other. As we might guess, because this president obliterated an important facet of the group's culture (collaboration), and also the institution's culture, leadership at this institution was, in a sense, paralyzed. People simply did not know how to act in the redefined setting.

Some leaders hold up team flaws like excessive cohesion as proof that teams are not a good idea, and they act on their findings by trying to wipe out the idea of teams altogether. We suggest that instead of destroying teams that are not working well, leaders should try to rebalance them. We discuss the relationship between teams and their larger institutions in chapters 5 and 7, and in chapter 8 we present suggestions for how to go about rebalancing team structure and process without destroying the team.

Teams May Inadvertently Fall into the Trap of Groupthink

The term *groupthink*, coined by Irving L. Janis (1972), refers to the phenomenon of "assumed consensus," which discourages individuals in a group from expressing their doubts or presenting disconfirming evidence (Morgan 1986). Briefly, groupthink keeps people from making critical observations or raising important questions. While such behaviors may have little effect in the short run, they may be disastrous over time.

Several factors contribute to groupthink. We tend to associate the words *team* and *teamwork* with harmony, consensus, and coordination, with people working together in an orderly and peaceful fashion to meet clearly established goals. When team members consciously or unconsciously avoid expressing rival viewpoints for fear of disturbing their team's harmony, the team falls into the trap of groupthink. For example, some members may defer to the opinion of others who express their views more readily and may refrain from dissent, question, or speculation beyond the stated views. Charismatic leaders may unintentionally produce groupthink by inspiring high degrees of confidence and perceptions of their invulnerability among colleagues and others who, because of the leader's convincing words and demeanor, come to doubt their own assessments of the situation at hand, particularly if that assessment is inconsistent with the leader's (Morgan 1986). We will return in chapter 4 to the concept of groupthink and how to counter it through an alternative dynamic, a process that we call "team thinking."

Teamwork May Actively Silence Different or Opposing Views

The ideology of teamwork emphasizes group consensus and shared understandings of reality. According to Rosabeth Moss Kanter (1983), "The mythology that surrounds the idea of 'team' . . . holds that differences among members do not exist—because now they are a 'team'— and, therefore, it is not legitimate to acknowledge them or talk about them" (p. 262). What results is often a pretense that people inside the team "do not see that some are more able than others, or that the highest-level people are dominating, or that the chair is railroading another decision through" (p. 262). Rather "everyone has to act as if they were all sharing equally in the operations of the group" (p. 262).

In our research we found that women, in particular, but also members of minority groups (although to a lesser extent in our study because there were so few in the sample), frequently felt out of synch with the rest of the group but that they rarely made their feelings known to the president or to other team colleagues. Gareth Morgan (1986) explains that an emphasis on harmony, including the team rituals, images, and symbols designed to enhance it, may blind a group to otherwise obvious differences in individual perspectives. In such cases teamwork can become superficial; individuals may pretend cooperation, usually by withholding dissent, even though they feel it. Silencing of this sort differs from groupthink, whereby individuals more willingly surrender the prerogative to question and to exercise their skills in critical thinking. We will return to a discussion of the dynamics of inclusion and exclusion within teams in chapters 6 and 7.

Teamwork Is Time Consuming

One reason why few leadership groups work well is that team development is extremely time consuming. Teamwork means much more than the conduct of a weekly meeting for the purpose of bringing people up to date on institutional matters. Team building requires great effort and attention from the president, vice president, dean, department chair, or director who truly desires a team that exhibits the advantages discussed earlier in this chapter and minimizes the disadvantages. The team builder must constantly work at converting a cluster of individual administrators, faculty members, or staff persons into a leadership team that embodies the advantages of teamwork and minimizes the disadvantages. This means that the team builder must devote time to questions such as:

- How should the team's agenda be constructed?
- Which items should be included in the agenda, and which should not?
- Who should participate in agenda building, and how?
- How flexible and changeable should the agenda be? How should change in a constructed agenda be handled?

It also means that the team builder (or team builders when several persons share the responsibility) should be skilled at involving group members in discussions. He or she should be able to observe and analyze group dynamics so as to be able to spot factors that facilitate or inhibit teamwork. The team builder should also know how to highlight those factors that improve the team's work process and to downplay or otherwise adjust the barriers to teamwork. Because such tasks are fraught with ambiguity and uncertainty (no two teams are fully alike), the team builder's job is highly demanding. Doing it well requires a high level of commitment and a steep investment of time. College presidents and other leaders typically have busy schedules, and they may believe that dedicating themselves to team development is not the most productive use of their time. Because the outcomes of teamwork are not quantifiable or, for that matter, fully understood, there is often little incentive among such people to dedicate time, thought, and effort to team building when numerous other more tangible and often more pressing tasks are at hand. One of our purposes in writing this book is to make teamwork a clearer, more understandable part of institutional life and thereby to improve the chance that leaders will give the quality of their teamwork the attention that we believe it deserves.

Team building is also time consuming because it is never ending. Because membership turnover is inevitable, we can think of teams as constantly remaking themselves. When a key member leaves, the team's functioning is likely to be impaired, sometimes irreparably. In our research interviews, the president of Blue Hills College, after rating her team a 10 (on a scale of 1 to 10), pointed out that the high rating represented the team's functioning prior to the recent resignation of a vice president who had played a key role on the team. She described the impact of his departure as follows: "The Vice President used to help. He and I modeled our relationship for the others. He and I would get into arguments and debate, and he would not relent. We showed that it was okay to argue with the President. They [the other team members] came to realize that I wanted to see a problem from all angles. That helped to open up what used to be a very repressive situation."

For the president of Blue Hills College, the vice president's departure was an overwhelming loss, and it represented an overwhelming compensatory task. Now, in addition to spearheading the search for a new vice president, she would have to begin the work of recreating the team. Once selected, the new vice president would have to learn the culture of the team already in place and how to work with it. The team, in return, would have to learn how to work with the newcomer, helping her or him become a part of the circle.

Recreating a team can take a great deal of energy on the part of the team builder. If the departed member was highly influential and valued, as was the vice president of Blue Hills College, then the team is likely to feel a strong sense of loss and vulnerability. Team members may expect the newcomer to fulfill the same role as the predecessor—to act, talk, think, and otherwise interact like the person who previously held the position. The group may also become angry at the newcomer who does not conform immediately to the implicit rules and norms of the group. Similarly, the newcomer may feel at a loss on discovering that the new job and the new institution differ from his or her former position, and especially on learning that the new team setting is something that must be learned and navigated with care.

The team builder (in the case of Blue Hills College, its president) is likely to feel responsible—and to be held accountable—for helping both parties, the old team and the new member, to adjust to each other and to coalesce. Nearly all of the presidents in our study were confronted with problems of membership turnover and team rebuilding during the course of their presidencies. And many expressed how difficult dealing with such problems directly could be. Many hoped that, with time, the problems would resolve themselves. At such points in a team's history, teamwork often became a disadvantage as the team turned into an arena where tension erupted.

Summary

Teams, team processes, and team histories are indeterminate. Teams are vulnerable. They take virtually ceaseless hard work. They can be an emotional drain. Unsurprisingly, some administrators believe that a team is more a liability than a help and choose to avoid the demanding work of team building. While we offer no prescriptions or formulas for making such work easier (as we have noted, we don't believe in them), we devote this book to stimulating knowledgeable and creative thought about how persons in leadership positions can develop teams that act and think as effectively as possible amid the unpredictable contingencies and seemingly insurmountable complexities of organizational life.

We begin this book with the assertion that leadership teams come in many shapes and forms, that they work in diverse ways, and that they serve diverse purposes. In presenting this array of team forms, functions, and purposes, we make the following points: that the concept of "team" has multiple meanings; that team builders bring unique models of leadership and teamwork to bear on their realities and, in doing so, reject other models; and finally, that the teamwork and leadership models they invoke shape their team's capabilities, accomplishments, concerns, and effectiveness.

2

A Different Way to
Think about Leadership Teams:
Teams as Cultures

As suggested in chapter 1, we believe that within the coming decades, conventional beliefs about what leadership means and how it works will give way to new conceptions, at least to conceptions that, to date, have remained under cover. Before we discuss what we believe to be the emerging view of leadership, particularly as it involves teams, we will briefly review conventional beliefs, many of which still prevail. In the second part of the chapter we will turn to the emerging view of teams as cultural entities.

A Review and Critique of Current Views of Leadership

Because a particular definition of leadership implies a corollary image of the organization within which leadership is exercised, theories of leadership vary as conceptions of organization vary (Bensimon, Neumann & Birnbaum 1989). For example, when we think of colleges or universities as *bureaucracies*, we imagine leaders as employing rational thought in making plans and decisions, as acting on the basis of logic, as getting expected results—or as correcting their action according to information provided through preestablished control systems. When we think of colleges or universities as *collegiums*, we see leaders engaged in the forging of consensus among multiple constituents or using interpersonal skills to manage processes of consultation. From a collegial perspective, a leader strives to meet people's needs and helps them realize their aspirations. When we consider institutions of higher education as *political systems*, we see leaders as mediators, negotiating among shifting power blocs and exerting influence through persuasion and diplomacy. Finally, when we view institutions as *symbolic systems*, and particularly as *organized anarchies* (Cohen & March 1974), we think of leaders as making modest improvements through unobtrusive actions and through manipulation of symbols (Birnbaum 1988, Bolman & Deal 1984). From the perspective of the organized anarchy, leaders are constrained by existing organizational structures and processes; thus they are generally capable of making only minute changes in the margins of their organizations (Birnbaum 1988).

While these models offer cogent explanations of how leadership is exercised, they are also quite limited in that they work from the assumption that leadership is the property of just one person rather than a group. For the most part, each of these models designates the individual as the primary unit of action and analysis. The models refer to the group (or network of leaders working together, intentionally or not, satisfactorily or not) only in a vague way—as a simple sum of the individuals who are presumably the more basic building blocks of organization. Viewed in terms of prevailing theories, the group, or web of leadership as Tierney (1988) has called it, is a secondary object that is, for the most part, underconceptualized in contemporary literature on leadership. That is, the leadership group, team, or "web" is largely undescribed, unexplored, and unmentioned. Despite assertions that groups, not persons, are likely to be the basic units of organization, we still barely know the group as an entity unto itself and as a fundamental building block of organization.

We have found that writers and researchers alike typically neglect the group not because they consider it worthless but because many have not yet learned to see, think, and talk about it as a phenomenon in and of itself—that is, as more than the sum of its parts. The individualistic (person-centered) base of contemporary leadership theory is inscribed and framed in the very language that we use to speak of leadership in organizations. For example, while we have countless words to describe how effective or ineffective certain individuals are in carrying out their leadership roles, we have virtually no vocabulary, nor do we have a syntax, to guide our talk and our thinking about leadership as a shared and interwoven dynamic spread simultaneously over many people in interaction.

The language or dominant discourse associated with the prevailing model of leadership sets one person (the leader) apart from the rest of the organization, asserting that this person provides a global perspective and direction that ensures the survival and progress of all (Bensimon 1991a). This assumption underlies most of the leadership frames in use today. For example, from the perspective of bureaucratic organization, this special person—the good leader—acts rationally. From a collegial perspective, the leader acts as the first among equals. Viewed politically, the leader is a power broker. Within the model of organized anarchy, the leader is merely an actor, albeit with special responsibilities, who adjusts reactively and incrementally to an overpowering stream of organizational life.

While models or frames such as these are insightful and provide us with ways to make sense of complicated organizational realities, they are based on beliefs that are antithetical to leadership that is truly shared in the sense that sharing implies inclusiveness. First and foremost, we see the prevailing models as inadequate because all of them cast leadership unequivocally as a quality of the individual rather than of the group. Second, the prevailing models emphasize what people have in common, or what they can come to have in common, through the "vision" of the individual leader. They thus detract attention from differences in how individuals construe the world, thereby favoring the dominant (commonly established or authority-centered) view over the private, personal perception and belief. This is the irony: While these models cast leadership as the quality of the individual, they simultaneously obscure what is uniquely individual among those who presume to follow the leader, favoring instead "the common view" espoused by the leader. While the person viewed as the team leader may feel satisfied in finding a common rubric for circumscribing the team's thinking and acting, this person often fails to face up to the fact that by virtue of the circumscription, team members are able to voice only part of their thinking within the team. Part of what each member knows, believes, and sees is likely to remain under cover. The danger to individuals caught in this kind of situation is that they are silenced; that is, their unique points of view are suppressed. The danger to the group is that it is likely to be caught in a narrow and inflexible mode of thinking that quickly becomes outdated.

Here is an example: While the collegial model of organization and leadership espouses many of the values associated with emerging conceptions of shared leadership, it assumes that words like "community," "scholar," and "academic" mean the same thing to all members of the academy. In assuming that all members have these definitions in common, it suppresses important differences in how individuals make sense of their world, for example, differences embedded in the minds of marginalized members of the academy, be they women, people of color, gay, lesbian, foreign born, or otherwise diverse by virtue of background and personal standpoint. For example, a woman, by virtue of her experiences as a woman, may construe *community* differently from its normative definition within a higher education system that was founded and long controlled by men—in effect, defined by them. In subscribing to the common, established view, which differs substantially from her native sense of what *community* means, the woman effectively suppresses her own view. This is the catch: This kind of suppression suggests that the entrenched definition of *community* will not be questioned and, therefore, that it will not change. Because she does not or cannot voice her unique point of view, this woman's perspective will probably make little difference in the configuration of her community, despite her presence within it. Moreover, because the community does not—or cannot—hear her, she is not likely to achieve full membership within it.

Differences in conception among people whose professional lives are generally lived in the margins of organization, away from dominant views, are often not obvious without careful listening, attention, and probing. It must also be recognized that when organizations fail to bring the voices of those who are at the margins to the center, the organization suffers. Moreover, a truly inclusive leadership is not possible without a mindful openness to such differences. What's the alternative?

The Emerging Imperative to Reconceptualize Leadership

We see the alternative to individual-centered leadership as leadership that is team oriented. Team-oriented leadership *assumes* that differences exist among people; it searches actively and affirmatively for them and seeks to bring them to light rather than insisting on talking only about the views that people share in common. The purpose of team-oriented leadership is to enlarge individual members' understandings of each other's views rather than insisting on a dominant but delimiting view, to encourage the expression of dissensus rather than emphasizing consensus, to bring out differences rather than looking mostly to similarities. Rather than looking for the overlaps in what we already know (thereby closing off exploration of what one team member might know that others do not know), team-oriented leadership seeks to bring people who differ face to face in open dialogue about what they believe, see, and experience. It encourages acceptance and learning, even of things that we do not yet know how to see. It fosters continued development of people's intrinsic differences, rather than covering them up. By focusing on differences rather than commonalities, team-oriented leadership helps to open our eyes to what others see that we have not previously been privy to. It helps us to learn, in the deepest sense of the word.

In order to remodel leadership so that it is truly team directed, leaders (whether presidents, deans, department chairs, directors, or others) will need to put aside the long-standing belief that leadership is a force for marshaling commonality and consensus to the point of excluding unique points of view and unique definitions of reality. Moreover, to conceive of leadership as a collective and interactive act, it is necessary to reconstruct our definitions of leadership, to build a "view of leadership which counters the emphasis on individualism, hierarchical relationships, bureaucratic rationality and abstract moral principles" (Blackmore 1989, p. 94) because all of these tend to exclude. Individualism blocks out connections to others; hierarchy suppresses that which is out of order; rationality is typically blind to emotional and nonrational processes; abstract morality misses the human particularity of everyday life.

Recent scholarship on the moral development of women merits consideration as a theoretical base for the reconceptualization of leadership as a collective and interactive act. This is because it is grounded in the experience of people—women—whose backgrounds differ dramatically from the norm of leadership, which is male dominated and heavily individualistic in orientation. We believe that this body of knowledge about women, about women's ways of knowing and thinking, and about efforts to liberate that thinking, is particularly relevant to a reconceptualization of leadership based on the theme of inclusive teamwork for the following reasons:

- Women, as a group, tend to define themselves—to establish their own identities—in terms of their relationships to others, as opposed to men, who typically establish identity through separation from others (Gilligan 1982; Gilligan, Lyons & Hanmer 1990).
- Women view themselves as interdependent, and they typically assess the merit of their work against standards of responsibility and care toward others. Men typically view themselves as independent and judge themselves and their work according to standards of individual achievement and competency (Ferguson 1984).
- Women perceive a world made up of physically and socially embodied "things," that are, by nature, continuous with one another and that are governed from within—for example, by internal wants and needs. Men construe a world of physically and socially disembodied "things" that are discrete and naturally independent of each other, though governed by uniform laws or principles of operation that may be manipulated by knowledgeable external agents (for example, by individuals in controlling positions) (Ferguson 1984). The women's perspective is

more conducive to the view of a team as a connected, living, thinking whole than the male view, which emphasizes control from the outside by a solo agent.

While we see these beliefs as undergirding how women make sense of their worlds, we do not mean to assert that the leadership practices of *all* women leaders have been shaped in identical ways by identical experiences. Nor do we mean to keep men from using these ideas or even from claiming them as equally their own. Our point is simply that this view is different from the conventional belief, which we see as more typically male, more typically separatist in orientation, and more exclusionary. The newer perspective, borrowed from studies of women's lives, emerges from an experience, that of women, which differs radically from the current norm of leadership based on men's experience of the social world. It emerges from a different sense of status. It emerges from a different sense of responsibility and relationship. While the perspective is grounded in research on women's experiences and moral development, we hope that both men and women will take from it and learn from it.

Jill Blackmore (1989) shows how the scholarship on women's moral development can be used to reconstruct the conventional model of leadership. Rather than conceiving of leadership as unidimensional and as posited within one individual, she advocates "a view of power which is multi-dimensional and multi-directional" (p. 94), drawing others into the center rather than subordinating, marginalizing, or excluding them. She asserts a new view of leadership that builds on the following beliefs:

Leadership can be practised in different contexts by different people and not merely equated to formal roles. (P. 94)

Leadership looks to empower others rather than have power over others. (P. 94)

Leadership is concerned with communitarian and collective activities and values. Thus the process of leading is both educative and conducive to democratic process. (P. 94)

Leadership, and the power which accompanies it, [may] be redefined as the ability to act with others to do things that could not be done by an individual alone. (P. 123)

The growing scholarship on the social experience and moral development of women gives us a lens for considering how leadership can be enacted, including the beliefs upon which the emerging team leadership theories rest, the values that they promulgate, and most importantly, the ends that they seek. We will return to the topic of feminist thought in relation to conceptions of team leadership in later chapters, but first we will delve more deeply into what the word *team* means. If, as we noted earlier, *team* has not yet been conceptualized beyond the sum of its individual parts, then how might we begin to make sense of it? What language might we use, borrow, or invent to help us talk and think about the team as the source, indeed the embodiment, of leadership, rather than looking only to individuals? We turn now to a definition of team as culture.

Rethinking What We Mean by Teams and Teamwork

If words are associated with thoughts, and if team-oriented leadership is, indeed, a thought that differs in important ways from previous individual-centered conceptions of leadership, what words should we use to capture its meaning and to describe how it works? After all, most of the words at our disposal relate to individualistic images of leadership.

Before we discuss the emerging image of the leadership team as a "culture," let us consider the prevailing image. Organizational theorists (e.g., Bolman & Deal 1991) and observers (e.g., Gilmore 1988) propose the athletic team as a metaphor for helping administrative leaders understand the structure and coordination of effective work groups. While the athletics-inspired team metaphor has gained widespread popularity in the corporate literature, we believe that, as a model for higher-education leadership teams and teamwork, it falls short on several counts.

One shortcoming of the athletic team metaphor is that it fosters a mechanistic view of groups. Athletic teams are extremely static in their structure. The roles of players are prescribed by their positions within the team and rarely shift. While the members of a leadership team may be just as static with regard to their roles within the institution (e.g., as vice president for student affairs, associate dean for business affairs, etc.), their roles within the team (which, as we will explain later, are not the same as their institutional roles) are more fluid and shared. For example, as we will describe in chapter 4, the members of leadership teams often play certain "thinking roles" among themselves, and while these roles may be constant within the team, they are not relegated to just one member. Any one person can play, or learn to play, any of the thinking roles. On leadership teams, the players' positions shift more quickly and unpredictably than on athletic teams.

Moreover, unlike athletic teams, where roles imply specific, self-contained actions for specific players (and thereby exclude others from certain plays), roles in leadership teams set off ripples of activity that engulf other team members, drawing virtually all of them into the activity that the person in the role merely set off. Let us consider a specific example. In baseball, when there are runners on base, an infielder fielding a ground ball always knows which base to throw to, and the outfielders may not be involved in the play at all. In a leadership team, the person in the team analyst role typically sets off a process of analysis that ripples across the team, drawing in all members (either in agreement or disagreement) but never purposefully excluding any. Unlike the infielder, the analyst does not merely execute the analysis for the team. Rather the analyst typically voices an analytic insight which she or he believes the team should consider. In doing so, this member *also* initiates a larger "analytic play" that is enacted by the team as a totality and in which different members often pull in different directions.

Another shortcoming of the athletic team metaphor is that it is inconsistent with the complex dynamics of leadership as teamwork. The internal processes of athletic teams are likely to be more rational and linear (in a word, simpler) than those of leadership teams because they emerge from and are guided by a single, incontestable goal—beating the opposing team. In contrast, leadership teams are held together not by a clear goal but by numerous interacting symbolic processes that provide a sense of unity and a feeling of direction. Moreover, in leadership teams, the game often generates the goals rather than the conventional reverse, and the opposition (assuming that there is such a thing) is unclear, or changeable at best (Weick 1979). For athletic teams the outcomes are visible and quantifiable: the team either wins or loses. For leadership teams the outcomes are fuzzier. Unlike the athletic team, whose game has a clear beginning and end, the leadership team is engaged in a continuous process. Nor does the leadership team come to closure at the end of the academic "season," count its wins and losses, and disperse until the next season.

A third shortcoming of the athletic team metaphor is that, in sports, just as in society at large, spectators tend to glorify the accomplishments of the individual player rather than considering the interactive work— both visible and invisible—of the collectivity. Sports fans fixate on the individual hero-athlete—his incredible feats, his unparalleled prowess. According to the headlines, it was not the spirit or dynamic of teamwork that brought victory to the Chicago Bulls. It was Michael Jordan—his artistry, creativity, airborne wizardry, and ability to control the flow of the game both on offense and defense—that led the team to win the 1991 and 1992 NBA championships. While we believe in the importance of talented, competent team members, we are more concerned with what

they do together and how they do it than with what each person contributes in a highly visible way. This, of course, is less a problem with
the athletic metaphor itself than with sports fans, who typically prefer
to ascribe success or failure to individuals rather than to interactive
processes—exactly the same problem that we typically encounter with
leadership teams when collegiate "spectators" choose one person (often
the president) to blame or praise rather than the work of the group as a
whole.

Just as in the leadership team, our language for talking about the
individual athlete's successes and failures is far better developed than our
language for talking about the team's interactive processes. Thus, in some
ways, the athletic team model suffers from the same conceptual problem
as the leadership team model in that it is typically interpreted in the
language of individualism rather than collectivity. A more fundamental
model, grounded in interaction, connection, and relationship is needed.

The Emerging Model: The Team as a Culture

Having discarded the athletic team as a potential model to guide our
analysis of leadership teams, we remain with the question: What, then,
is a good model to help us think about what team-oriented leadership
is, how it works, and what we might expect to gain from it? Let us begin
by noting the significance of the words, *model, lens, frame, image*, and
personal theory, which for the purpose of this explanation we lump
together.

We have already noted that theorists as well as organizational participants (e.g., administrators, faculty members, trustees, and so forth) make
sense of institutional events by subjecting them to theoretical lenses that
are uniquely theirs (Gioia 1986). We have found, in our previous studies,
that presidents (and others) carry in their heads an array of personal
theories about the nature of organization and leadership (Bensimon 1989,
Neumann 1989, Neumann & Bensimon 1990). The theories may be
obvious—that is, used openly and consciously—or they may be latent—
present but unarticulated. These theories serve as screens or windows to
let certain things into our minds and keep certain things out and to ascribe
to the vast quantity of stimuli around us a certain order and sense of
causality in the world (see Bensimon, Neumann & Birnbaum 1989, Birnbaum 1988, Bolman & Deal 1984). Our point is that, while presidents,
administrators, and others typically exhibit a variety of theories, models,
or lenses in their thoughts about leadership and in their exercise of leadership, many share the tendency to ascribe leadership to just one person

at a time. We believe that this is, in fact, the prevailing view in the field
and the current state of the art. While leadership manifests itself in diverse
forms, showing a variety of faces (bureaucratic, collegial, political, symbolic, and so forth), its base structure is fairly uniform and consistent
(focused on the individual actor).

It is the nature of this individualistic base that we are most concerned
with. In searching for a new model for team leadership, we look for
words and images that can help us escape the pattern of individually
centered ideas, words, and sentences that currently guide (and limit) our
thoughts. We look for a new base language, a revised "root metaphor"
(Smircich 1983) that purposefully seeks to conceptualize the shape, spirit,
dynamics, and meaning of the whole. It is in this spirit that we re-present
the leadership team as a culture.

When we apply the metaphor of culture to the leadership team, we
envision a web of actors connected to one another through norms, beliefs,
rituals, values—that is, through meaning that they continually construct
and reconstruct. Rather than focusing on team "results," with attention
to the virtuoso performances of the specific "players" who presumably
achieve them, our attention is on how team members interact with or
distance themselves from one another, how they share or withhold power
in decision making, and how they use language to give meaning to their
interactions and to their sense of interrelatedness. From a cultural perspective, we try to interpret and understand how group members work
together and how the group functions as a collectivity, rather than focusing on individual performances only. By comparison with the athletic team
metaphor, the culture metaphor better captures the image (and, thereby,
gives us a language) of community. It helps us conceptualize the team as
much more than the simple sum of the individuals belonging to it.

A caveat is in order. The word *culture* can be read in two different ways.
It may be viewed functionally, as an organizational attribute or variable
that is assessable, for example, as weak or strong. Writers who work in
this vein typically urge managers to "get a handle" on their group's or
organization's culture in order to assume control of its stability (see
Morgan 1986). This functionalist view (Burrell & Morgan 1979) suggests
that culture is something that a team *has* rather than what a team *is*.
From a functionalist perspective, culture is a tool that managers can
manipulate toward desired ends. It assumes that managers work rationally from clearly thought-out goals or objectives, and that they have the
power to maneuver and even transform cultures in line with their goals.

Emerging perspectives question these functionalist assumptions. Recent
studies show that managers rarely work rationally from prestated goals

and that goals typically serve rather as rationalizations derived retrospectively, after action is complete (Weick 1979), or emerge in the very process of action (Schon 1983). The emerging perspective also makes the point that cultures are not as manipulable as the functionalist perspective implies and that they are anything but managerial tools. In fact, a number of recent studies show that organizational cultures may overwhelm—even overpower—managers, a lesson that many new college presidents seem to learn only "the hard way" (Neumann 1990a, Neumann 1991a).

This is the fundamental point: We do not conceive of teams as organizational objects with culturelike attributes. Such objects are not cultures at all; they are something different, even though they look or act like cultures. This mistranslation of the culture concept throws us right back to the conventional, functionalist view of the team as a managerial tool. Now the team, still a managerial tool to its core, simply dresses up like a culture! In taking the opposing position—that a team *is*, in fact, a culture to its core—we authentically revise our root metaphor, turning culture into our base lens for making sense out of life in teams.

We also want to establish that, in choosing the word *culture* to capture the meaning of *team*, we do not mean to direct our readers' attention purely toward integrative factors—for example, the cultural rituals, symbols, stories, and patterns of language that lend consistency (or a common story line) to team members' values, interpretations and assumptions about life in their college, most of which are likely to vary dramatically from person to person (Frost et al. 1991). To the contrary, while our perspective acknowledges that integrative and sense-making processes abound in teams viewed as cultures, it assumes that cultural fracturing is at work as well—whether in the form of communication breaks, power inequities, gender biases, status differences, or a host of other imbalances, tensions, and contradictions (Frost et al. 1991). We believe that because team members bring a variety of perspectives, experiences, and beliefs to their work, a team is as likely to fracture under its own weight as it is to become cohesive in its cognitive complexity.

While the team's cognitive diversity promises creativity born of complexity, it also bodes difficult clashes and gaps in understanding among team members, and also between the team and other organizational constituencies. In sum, our perspective on teams as cultural entities considers both consistency and difference, cohesion and fragmentation, creation and degeneration, unity and fragmentation. It considers how teams come together, grow together, and stay together, but it also examines the dynamics of their coming apart.

In this book, we use the culture metaphor to reconceptualize the leadership team, in much the same way that others (Meyerson & Martin

1987, Smircich 1983) have used it to transform traditional, functionalist views of organizations into images of organizations as relational and interpretive webs of constructed meaning. Let us consider a brief illustration of what it means to view a team as a cultural entity—as a body that simultaneously coheres and fractures in its meaning, relationships, and work dynamics. One approach to reconceptualizing teams from a cultural perspective is to view them as narratives that we must "read" or decipher (Smircich 1983) from the various perspectives of the multiple author-actors who create them and who, in telling us their stories in extensive interviews, give us their particular versions of the narrative. Our "reading" of the team strives to discern how team members see, experience, and otherwise feel the realities that they and others have participated in creating, giving particular attention to the differences in the experiences of each. Thus we purposefully turn our attention away from what we are likely to see as visitors to the team (though we acknowledge that our own lenses are apt to get in the way), focusing instead on what the people on the team see, hear, and feel by virtue of their individual experiences. Again, we look at themes of both consistency and difference. The following example catches a cultural glimpse of life within the Dryland College team.

The team of Dryland College was exemplary in its performance as an institutional leadership group. Both in the college and on the team, morale and energy were at an all-time high. The college's financial condition was excellent. Innovation was in the air. Governance processes worked peacefully and productively. College leaders respected the faculty, and the faculty, in turn, admired their administrators, particularly the president. The team itself was cognitively diverse; it was particularly creative in defining and addressing problems. It was most supportive of the president's endeavors. Its members were action oriented and responsible; they got things done on their own and together. However, despite the obvious strengths of top-level administrative teamwork at Dryland College, there were also some deep-rooted conflicts that we might have missed (or simply dismissed) had we not searched actively for inconsistencies, differences, and contradictions in how people made sense of their collegiate world. Sometimes the inconsistencies were blatant; at other times they were more subtle.

In addition to the president, a man, we interviewed three other men and two women on the team; these five individuals held similar titles although their responsibilities fell in different areas. A "high-status" man on the team drew our attention to a rift in the group when he described the two women on the team as "struggling to bring things to the team so that they can have a sense of self-importance."

Let us begin our cultural "reading" of this team by examining the images that the high-status man evoked as he spoke these words. First, this man's statement reflects undertones of annoyance and disparagement. The two revealing phrases are "struggling" and "sense of self-importance." The reference to "struggle" suggests that the women are not as adept at bringing meaningful issues to the team as others (men) might be. Moreover, if the women had to struggle, those who were more competent (i.e., the men, who were not depicted as struggling) had to wait for them, and in the real time of managerial life this amounted to waste or at least to annoyance. The allusion to a "sense of self-importance" suggests three interpretations: (a) because the women were attempting to aggrandize themselves they were not "team players"; (b) because they were caught up in the task of *establishing* their importance, their value to the team was, by definition, yet unestablished; and (c) they were more concerned with establishing a "sense" (read "appearance") of importance than with real, instrumental utility. A deep cultural reading of the high-status man's words reveals the existence of animosity within this exemplary team, at least between this individual and the two women, an observation that we confirmed through other comments that he made: "She [a vice president] brings the largest volume of things to the group. She will always have something. The other one [another vice president] is similar, but sometimes she also uses the group to pursue her hidden agenda, especially regarding authority or control. She will want to keep her domain and bring into it what she can."

While the team at Dryland College works extraordinarily well at one level, it is troublesome at another. We would guess that animosities or annoyances, such as those expressed by the high-status man, would manifest themselves in the team's working relationships. Had we focused only on what makes this team effective at just one level, we would have missed a significant portion of the story. A cultural perspective invites the "reader" to delve beneath surfaces of seeming consistency in search of differences and disruptions. In the case of Dryland College the pattern of inconsistency points out that within the team, two women were trying to position themselves in relation to a very powerful and highly influential male colleague. In part this involved efforts to assume at least some control over the team's agenda. The high-status male member saw this as an irritating faux pas, and his words reflected his resentment. He described the women as "not knowing any better" and he discounted them: "They [the women] shouldn't try to dominate the team. They should realize that even though we [males on the team] listen politely, that's it. We do not take what is being said very seriously."

What kept this team from falling apart? A cultural analysis shows that the president of Dryland College knew about the conflict and its causes, and that he used his understanding of the personalities and the context to manage the conflict so as to balance the team's strengths with its difficulties. For example, the president understood that one of the two women on the team was especially "prone to want to push [the team] in new directions." He also understood that the men on the team were more conservative and viewed this woman's initiatives not as efforts to spur innovation but as attempts to "control the agenda." The president explained that, in cases such as this, he intercedes actively: "I have to be sensitive to group relationships that are not working, . . . to tell people how their personalities are creating difficulty." He managed the conflict in part by mirroring to team members how they looked and felt to others on the team and also by fostering a highly democratic climate. That is, he listened to his team colleagues. He also encouraged others to listen, either directly or, as in this case, indirectly—that is, through him as he explained to team members how their words or actions were making others feel. A male member of the team said that the president "is very careful to protect or guard that everyone is always equal, that we can say what is on our minds, that our opinions are equally valued." It is no surprise that the two women on the team agreed with this description.

The conflict between the high-status man and the two women occurred in one of the best of our teams—one judged as thinking complexly (Neumann 1991c) and as fulfilling multiple functions as needed (Bensimon 1991b)—and it involved an exemplary president, one defined as cognitively complex (Bensimon 1989), sensitive to interpretive differences and exhibiting interpretive skill (Neumann 1989), oriented toward learning (Neumann 1990a), and attuned simultaneously to internal and external pressures, demands, and changes (Neumann & Bensimon 1990).

A cultural analysis helps us look not only at patterns of success and agreement in organizations but also at patterns of hardship and contradiction (Chaffee & Tierney 1988). It helps us understand that reality is more than just one thing—that it exists in layers, and that until the layers are peeled away we have only a partial picture of what is happening. Thus teams (and also organizations) that appear to be working exceedingly well on one level may shield stressful rifts, conflicts, or contradictions inside the team (Neumann 1992). These often manifest themselves only as background noise and as secondary to the "real" and substantive issues on the administrative agenda. To get to them, we first had to sort through the massive, concrete details of life at this college. While it was hard for *us* to see—and also admit to—the blemishes on our exemplary team, imagine how much more difficult it is for presidents and other administrators to be completely aware of all that may be happening around them.

Sometimes it is easier for someone like the president of Dryland College to leave conflicts under cover than to encourage open dialogue about them. Although we know that the president of Dryland College "managed" the latent conflict on his team indirectly, he did not, to the best of our knowledge, name it openly within the team, which would have made it a reality that his colleagues on the team could address as well as he. We mention this not to be critical but rather to emphasize a point to which we will return in later chapters: that even when conflict is acknowledged (in many teams it is not), it is rarely put on the table as a subject for team dialogue.

Suppressing discussions about conflict arising from interpersonal differences is confining. Interpersonal conflict inevitably involves feelings— the personal stuff that tends to be categorized as private and, therefore, as untouchable professionally. In the common professional view, emotions typically preclude facts and are often deemed out of place in the public (and professional) realm of teams. But in excluding consideration of emotions, teams and team leaders limit their understandings of what is happening around them. They also cut short the range of actions they might take.

A cultural perspective promises to help teams come to terms with their internal, unspoken differences in that it seeks to make those differences explicit. As Linda Smircich (1983) says, "A cultural analysis moves us in the direction of questioning taken-for-granted assumptions, raising issues of context and meaning, and bringing to the surface underlying values" (p. 355), many of which differentiate us from one another. Because it encourages reflexivity—defined as the unearthing and critical examination of assumptions and values—the culture metaphor stands as an improvement on convention: It gets behind behaviors, externalities, and outcomes and probes instead the thinking, knowing, and feeling of people's experiences within their organizational worlds (Neumann, in press c). The athletic team metaphor is limiting in a very critical way: it speaks only to the physical or objective side of "coordinated doing." In contrast, the culture metaphor "focuses attention on the expressive, non-rational qualities of the experience," and "it legitimates attention to the subjective, interpretive aspects" of group life (Smircich 1983, p. 355). To view the team in this way—as a reflexive, cultural entity—is "to emphasize its humanness" (Greenfield 1984, p. 143) over its functional objectivity. We will say more about these two dimensions of team life, and the importance of getting inside how teams think and know, in the next chapter.

What the Culture Metaphor
Can Mean to College Leaders

The culture metaphor has been extremely helpful to researchers concerned with understanding life in groups and in organizations generally. We believe that it can be just as helpful to administrators and other leaders desiring to improve their own and their colleagues' performance. But the acquisition of cultural competence is no simple task. It requires, first and foremost, the loosening and unlearning of the functionalist perspective. This is what is at the heart of reconceptualized leadership. When it comes to understanding teams, the functionalist perspective cannot exist side by side with the cultural. As a first step, reconceptualization involves accepting and knowing, at a definitive level, *what a team is not*:

- A team is not a physical object that comes to life on the basis of clearly prescribed roles.
- It is not a rational structure acting intentionally to achieve prespecified ends.
- It is not a machinelike entity that can be analyzed purely in terms of the discrete behaviors of its members.
- It is not a tool that managers can use to further their ends.

Reconceptualization also involves accepting a new understanding of the team—*what, in fact, a team is*:

- A team is a collectivity that is an entity in and of itself rather than merely the sum of its individual member parts.
- It is a set of actions, cognitions, feelings, and experiences.
- It is a setting marked by both shared and fractured meaning.
- It is a social reality created and recreated by those who are part of it.
- It is a reality that exists inside the head of each member—and, therefore, it is likely to differ, at least somewhat, from member to member. It is, therefore, a complex and often inconsistent reality.
- It is a reality that may be grasped only through close interpretation of the experiences and understandings of its individual members.
- It is a fluid set of beliefs, understandings, and differences—some consistent and complementary, others inconsistent and contradictory—encompassing members and exceeding them even as they create and recreate meaning, conflict, and ambiguity.

In order to achieve an understanding of the team as a cultural entity, college leaders should be able to interpret and understand their group's themes (including its mood), the nature of intragroup relations, and the norms that guide decision making and action. Persons who assume a cultural perspective vis-à-vis the team typically focus on whether and how the team's members think and act together; they are especially concerned with patterns of participation, including patterns of inclusion and exclusion (Chaffee & Tierney 1988). In this book we consider these factors by examining the functions that teams serve (chapter 3), the process of team thinking through a variety of interactive thinking roles (chapter 4), and the kinds of cultural skills that can help collegiate leaders interpret their teams and give meaning to teamwork (chapter 6).

3

What Teams Can Do: How Leaders Use—and Neglect to Use—Their Teams

In this chapter, we describe how the fifteen college and university presidents participating in our study made use of their teams. We compare presidents who involved their teams broadly in institutional affairs, giving team members a huge share of responsibility and authority in the thinking, feeling, and doing of leadership, with the presidents who saw leadership as a more restricted dynamic, making individual team members responsible for "segments" of institutional leadership rather than making them aware of larger wholes. We saw the former set of presidents as adhering to the view of the team as a cultural whole and the latter set as adhering to the more conventional view of a team as composed of segments that are merely summed together.

It has been suggested that college presidents have an all but impossible job (Birnbaum 1989), in part because their control of organizational resources is often illusory (Cohen & March 1974). Top-level leadership teams, particularly the president's cabinet or inner circle of administrative colleagues, may represent one of the few resources over which presidents in fact have some influence. On the basis of our study, we believe that a college's top-level leadership team can be an important resource for its president. Our discussions with a variety of people in administrative positions other than the presidency lead us to believe that teams can also be an important resource for vice presidents, college deans, department chairs, and other institutional leaders. However, we also believe that presidents and other leaders need to understand the nature of that resource—for example, how teams work, what they can do, and what they cannot do.

Our research suggests that while many presidents acknowledge the usefulness of their teams in a general way, often because intuitively they believe that teams are important, they frequently have trouble explaining exactly how or why they are useful. Some presidents, in fact, take their institution's top leadership group (i.e., their administrative circle) for granted without giving much thought as to how well it is working. Some presidents are oblivious to serious team dysfunctions that some of their vice presidents, and even many faculty, see clearly. We believe that because most presidents, and most people in leadership positions generally, lack a conceptual map of the functions that teams can fulfill, they may tend *not* to utilize their teams as fully as they might. In the next section we present a three-part framework for thinking about the functions of leadership teams.

To reiterate the point we made in chapter 2, we do not see these functions as restricted to or focused on particular individuals on the team but as encompassing the team as a total unit. At the same time, it is important to consider the fact that the individuals on the team are likely to shape its nature depending on whether they take a cultural or a conventional approach to thinking about it. Given the president's often prominent role as a team builder, we turn now to the question of how presidents conceive of their teams' functions.

Three Functions of Presidential Teams

One of the major findings of this study is that presidents who are effective team builders think in complicated ways about their team's work. In an analysis of how the fifteen presidents in this study view their teams, Estela Mara Bensimon (1991b) discovered that they construe the work of their teams in terms of three functions: utilitarian, expressive, and cognitive.* She pattern-coded (Miles & Huberman 1984) presidents' descriptions of their teams, utilizing the following question as a guiding frame: "In what ways does President X find his/her team useful?" The analysis yielded the three functions that we present, with specific examples, in this chapter. Table 3.1 also summarizes the findings of Bensimon's study.

---

*The following discussion elaborates on a research report by Estela Mara Bensimon titled, "How College Presidents Use Their Administrative Groups: Real and Illusory Teams," *Journal for Higher Education Management* 7 (1991): 35–51.

Table 3.1
Three Functions of Presidential Teams

Team Function	Image	Purpose	Behavior	Activities
Utilitarian	Formal	Help president achieve a sense of rationality and maintain control over institutional functioning	Task related	Deliver information, coordinate and plan, make decisions
Expressive	Social	Help reinforce a sense of groupness or connectedness among individuals involved in a joint venture	Integrative, associative	Provide mutual support, provide counsel to the president
Cognitive	Sense making	Enlarge span of intelligence of individual team members, enable the group to behave as a creative system and also as a corrective system	Intellective, dialogical	View problems from multiple perspectives; question, challenge, argue; act as monitor and feedback system

The Team's Utilitarian Function

From a utilitarian perspective, presidents view their teams as formal structures for achieving "rational organization" and for maintaining control over institutional functioning. Viewed as a utilitarian tool, the presidential team keeps the institution running and gets necessary jobs done. Moreover, it is purposive and task-oriented, engaging in instrumental activities such as: (*a*) providing information, (*b*) coordinating and planning, and (*c*) making decisions. While we define these three activities below, we also highlight the fact that each activity may manifest itself in more than one way.

PROVIDING INFORMATION

Depending on a president's orientation, the act of providing information can be an educative activity (information sharing), or it can serve as a perfunctory recital of facts that the "president needs to know" to avoid being surprised (information delivery).

In our study, the presidents who viewed this informational activity as *educative* were typically concerned with how "news" would affect the team as a whole, rather than just the president. As one president put it, "The team plays an important role in getting each other up to speed," and he described the team's information-sharing ritual of "going around the table and giving progress reports." Another president added that this kind of information sharing is important not only for instrumental reasons but because it is "important [that] we all hear certain things together." The presidents who spoke from the educative standpoint usually saw new information as an opportunity to establish a common ground for decision making.

In contrast, presidents who saw the provision of information more as an act of "delivery"—as a means for keeping *themselves* aware of institutional events—tended not to worry as much about the team's understanding of collegiate issues. These presidents portrayed themselves as individuals who were uncomfortable with the "unexpected," and they saw information delivery as a means of assuring that they (as individuals) would always have a ready response to whatever institutional difficulty confronted them. They were less concerned with a team response, including what that would look like in the public eye, than with their own personal response and what *they* would look like.

These presidents usually construed information as a resource over which they needed to establish control. They were apt to let their teams know (as one of our presidents did) that "being kept informed is a sacred matter" to them. One of the presidents we interviewed told the members of his team, "I have a right to the information in your brain; . . . to withhold information, . . . not to be candid with me is a cardinal sin."

The presidents oriented toward information delivery described themselves as possessing a team, but unlike the presidents who were concerned with the educative aspects of information provision, they typically did not see the team as a leadership group. Rather, they saw it as a "doing" group, and one of the things that they saw their group "doing" was connecting the president to the campus. In fact, these presidents often saw the team as their *only* connection to the campus. In their determination to stay connected—to know and see it all—these presidents would often assume a highly authoritarian tone as they demanded information from their vice presidents.

Teams that work this way—whose dominant function is the delivery of information to the president for the president's own benefit—cannot be regarded as real teams because they just provide information, without talk or input. Information provision is always a critical team activity. The challenge for presidents who are concerned with building truly effective teams is not to allow informational activity to become the sole reason for regular meetings of their administrative group.

In our study, presidents who limited the team's role to information delivery were a source of unhappiness for many of their administrative officers. A vice president on one of these teams put his concerns this way:

> I guess the most important thing is hearing what goes on at meetings at the state system level, but this is not necessarily what should be going on. Ideally I would like to see it [the team meeting] as a place [where] institution-wide issues could be discussed with a certain amount of candor. A team needs to know the major issues. While I do not have responsibility for academic programs I should be able to contribute my ideas. There should be open debate. The institution benefits from different perspectives. We also need to examine, jointly, where our energies are going. But rarely are those issues introduced. We are just informed when something is brought to the table. If you venture too far out of your territory you are told so.

In sum, this vice president saw information delivery as a constraining activity that impinged on open and creative team thinking and team learning.

To summarize, we agree with yet another interviewee who quietly told us, "If the purpose of team meetings is to keep the president on top of what is happening, there are probably a lot [of] better ways of doing that than through a weekly cabinet meeting."

COORDINATION AND PLANNING

Teams that were active in goal setting and strategic planning for the purpose of institutional coordination, a utilitarian aim, generally did not limit members to their official areas of responsibility and expertise (e.g., academic affairs or student affairs). Rather, they sought to involve team members, regardless of their divisional responsibilities, in the "crafting of an institutional agenda that [was] representative of all constituent parts."

As one president pointed out, "The key thing about the annual goals statement [is that it is the outcome of extensive] consultation with the group." Another president asserted his belief that the team's involvement in institutional goal setting was important in that it avoided "disparity" among the vice presidents with regard to where they saw "the institution going." In the words of the president, "Everyone knows what is the most important driving force." He added that, as a result of their participation in the making of the "institutional agenda," team members felt more committed to it.

The majority of presidents in our study were quick to recognize their team's usefulness for coordination and planning in the abstract sense, but when we asked them to elaborate with examples or explanation, many were unclear as to how the coordination and planning actually occurred. Additionally, not all presidents were aware of the practical and symbolic advantages of team involvement in broad-based campus matters (e.g., via strategic planning). One president said that his team was "least useful" in terms of "long-range issues, such as where the institution should be five or ten years from now." For this president, the team was more useful for specific, short-range issues such as determining "how an action in one area may influence other areas" and then adjusting accordingly. But this president saw the team's contribution to other matters—particularly if they were out of the ordinary—as wasteful and uncomfortable, mainly because he feared that the diversity of the individuals involved would lead to a "loss of coherence." He pointed out to us that the campus's best long-range planners were himself and the executive vice president, and he excluded all other team members from all but the most basic of administrative functions.

DECISION MAKING

Another important activity related to the team's utilitarian function is decision making. In this study this was particularly true among presidents who had adopted consensus procedures within the team whereby each member had a significant voice and sometimes a vote. A consensus approach to decision making was particularly useful in assessing policy issues affecting the whole institution or in the allocation of financial resources. According to one president, "When decisions involve money, we hash it out in the group. Together we decide whether hiring a new counselor is more important than adding a new faculty member."

Decision making frequently involved giving members a formal say in the final decision, but this was not always the case. We found several utilitarian teams in which team members contributed to decision making in a more distanced advisory sense. For example, they provided the president with ideas, suggestions, and alternatives for consideration, but it was clear that the final decision would be made by the president. As one president told us, "We do not vote. After I have heard all I need to on an issue, I will come to a decision and I will set the assignments."

Although decision making would appear to be a critical administrative activity for a presidential team, surprisingly few presidents in our study considered their teams useful, in terms of either voting or giving advice, in this activity. We believe the presidents undervalued the teams' decision-making usefulness because they viewed group decision making negatively.

For example, some admitted to not "having the patience" required for decision making by consensus. Others viewed consensus as "a way in which individuals can avoid responsibility." Still others shied away from this kind of decision making because they felt that it made them appear indecisive or overly dependent on others. As one president put it, "You should be able to tie your own shoes."

We disagree. Our belief is that decision making can be enhanced when it is approached as a collaborative effort. We recognize, however, that the president's team is not the institution's supreme decision-making body. Other decision-making groups, most prominently the board of trustees, play important roles. We also recognize that the consensus model, as we commonly think of it, may be flawed. We pursue these points further in chapter 6.

The Team's Expressive Function

To develop the team's expressive function, presidents need to view their team as a social structure aimed at meeting team members' needs for collegial relations and affiliation as well as the president's needs for counsel and commitment. Through the expressive function, a team reinforces its sense of "groupness" or internal connectedness. We believe that "groupness" is important because it comprises the setting or ground on which the substantive work of collaboration may occur.

Our study identified two key activities that fall within the expressive domain of team functioning: (a) providing mutual support, and (b) providing counsel to the president.

PROVIDING MUTUAL SUPPORT

The capacity of the presidential team to provide mutual support was the expressive activity mentioned most often by the presidents in our study. Presidents said that it is important for the institution's top leadership group to "have a coherent chemistry" so that its members can be "supportive of one another in achieving the goals of the university." When administrative officers "have problems in their own areas," it is reassuring to them—and to their president—to know they are able "to get help from others on the team." Because top-level administrators have "lonely jobs," said one president, they need to act as "a support group for each other."

Some interviewees described the team as a place to go when campus life became particularly hard to take: "Faculty and students cannot appreciate some of the torment we go through. You are always confronted with the lack of resources, silly rules, . . . so if you do not have a group of people with whom you can laugh you can get burned out in administration." Others described the team as simultaneously creative and supportive: "The meetings have an agenda. We follow a certain form. But we also share our dreams, clear the air, compliment each other. That is the free-flowing creative aspect—it helps us all. I can rely on each of them to support me and not to become an adversary."

Our sample also contained several presidents who were uncomfortable with the expressive function, including the provision of mutual support. These presidents were very open in telling us that they did not want to "personalize relationships" on the team and preferred "to emphasize the responsibilities of the office." Our view, however, is that presidents who think this way are, in effect, forcing an artificial split between the personal and the professional and that, in doing so, they contribute to the suppression of connectedness. We do not believe that collaborative work, particularly collaborative thinking, can occur in thin air. We believe, instead, that such work requires a solid base of patterned interdependencies—a team that becomes the *setting* within which collaborative teamwork may occur.

We conclude from this that teams need to strive for relationships that consist of more than politically expedient alliances among individuals with different values and desires. For a group to exist there needs to be groupness.

PROVIDING COUNSEL TO THE PRESIDENT

While one would think that presidents would view their administrative groups as playing an important counseling role, our study suggests that few actually do. Among the presidents in our study who saw the team as their primary advisory group, one said, "I use the group as a sounding board. . . . If I don't have background on an issue, I lean on them for counsel." A second added, "They are there to guide and advise me."

Apart from offering substantive, instrumental advice to their president, the team can act as a mirror: team colleagues can provide presidents with feedback that lets them see themselves as others do. Presidents (especially new presidents) often want to know how they are doing, that is, how others see them, and their teams are a key source of this sort of information. One president said, "They [the presidential team] are expected to be candid and frank with me with regard to my leadership." Teams can also prevent presidents from taking action that would damage their leadership image. One president said, "I express my dependency on staff quite openly. I count on them not to let me go off on a crazy tangent. It is helpful to have people tell the emperor he has no clothes. I'd rather be foolish in a small group than in a large group."

Obviously, the extent to which top-level leadership teams can fulfill the role of counselor to the president depends heavily on whether the president-team relationship is based more on intimacy and collegiality than on purely official ties. The team's ability to fulfill a counseling role also requires a president who is able to rely strongly and openly on the team, to recognize that doing it all alone is impossible. Such presidents must also be willing to open thenselves to scrutiny. Not all presidents can accept such terms. In fact, many of the presidents in this study preferred to establish relationships based on loyalty rather than on interdependence.

Although a relationship based on loyalty need not preclude a counseling role for the institution's top leadership team, the concept of "loyalty to the president" communicates stiffness, and it connotes a rigid president-team relationship. When presidents talk of loyalty, they mean that the group has "to identify with the president" or "protect the president" or "be ready to sacrifice themselves" for the president's needs. The biggest difference between "counseling the president" and "showing loyalty to the president" is that the former suggests a relationship between peers and colleagues, while the latter is a demonstration of commitment by subordinates to a superior.

It is also important to distinguish between loyalty to an individual and loyalty to an institution. The former refers to team members' loyalty to the president alone, while the latter refers to their loyalty to the group. Loyalty to an institution may involve showing support for decisions that the group has made, or it may involve taking responsibility, both for wise choices and for choices made in error. Finally, the concept of loyalty suggests that each team member works "for the good of something." In the case of loyalty to an institution, this may require one or more team members to bring bad news to the group (for example, bring up something the team would prefer not to hear or deal with) or to be constructively critical of an idea within the group despite the group's attachment to the idea.

We conclude this section with a warning: highly associative teams risk insularity. They may inadvertently distance themselves from the rest of the campus. Thus, while a team may feel that it is engaged in collaborative decision making, the rest of the campus can feel left out. It sometimes takes a newcomer to the team to recognize that this is happening: "The few people on the cabinet were in agreement," said a new president, "but they failed to produce a consensus on campus." An interviewee on another campus described what he saw as his team's predicament:

We are not great in communicating to the rest of the campus, . . . telling them what is going on and what the direction is. The president does try to do this by writing memos and through faculty meetings. I think that there is a tremendous consensus among us [the team] on the institutional purpose and the philosophy. We have a shared sense of purpose. We understand that what each of us does affects the others. But communicating that outside, . . . we are very bad at doing that.

The Team's Cognitive Function

Presidents are likely to find the cognitive function to be the most challenging, if not the most problematic, to develop within the team. Yet of the three functions, this is without doubt the most critical. Our studies suggest that in order to bring the cognitive function into being, a president must view the institution as a complex system in which the team is the sense maker—that is, its members are collectively involved in perceiving, analyzing, learning, and thinking. Simply put, in its cognitive function the team is a brainlike social structure that enlarges the intelligence span of individual team members. Intellectual expansion allows the group to behave as a creative system when unusual events occur, and as a warning and corrective system in the case of dysfunction.

The team's cognitive function comprises mostly intellective and analytical activity, including: (a) viewing problems from multiple perspectives, (b) questioning, challenging, and arguing, and (c) acting as a monitor and feedback system.

Unless presidents make clear that they expect and welcome substantive and analytical questions and issues within the context of the team, the cognitive function may be compromised. For example, a highly influential member of one of our sample teams informed us that even though he brings many issues to the group, he never "brings anything without checking with the president first." Undoubtedly, this preliminary tête-à-tête between the president and the vice president risks undermining the team's cognitive usefulness. We would hope that presidents would actively discourage this "checking it out first with the president" form of behavior.

VIEWING PROBLEMS FROM MULTIPLE PERSPECTIVES

According to the presidents who defined the usefulness of their teams in cognitive terms, the most widely valued cognitive activity is generating multiple, diverse perspectives on problems at hand. Even though presidents consider it important for their teams to have a "common sense of the institution's values, its vision, its purposes, its goals and its priorities," they also expect their teams to produce "varying ideas on how to accomplish those things." As one president put it, "I would hope that [team members] would not all be clones of myself or anyone else—that they [would] be individuals in their own right."

Effective presidential teams act in ways that allow problems or issues to be examined from multiple points of view and along more than one value dimension. By bringing "individual [members'] perspectives" to bear on an issue, and by "suggesting alternative courses of action," these teams can be very useful in expanding the ways in which presidents come to view their institutions' special circumstances or problems. As one of the study presidents explained, "The team brings more ideas to me than I bring to them." Another president described how he looks to the team to be sure that all possible perspectives on an issue have been tried out and that all problem-solving options have been explored: "Usually only two or three alternatives may be considered, when in reality there is a fourth and a fifth. . . . I find that once these other alternatives are raised, an issue is more complicated than I realized, and strategies that I had not envisioned suddenly become evident."

Reconsidering a problem through multiple lenses might make the problem look more complex and might make a person feel that the problem is becoming less and less manageable. However, as a problem unfolds in its largeness, looking frighteningly more complicated all the time, its previously hidden facets may suggest solutions not seen when it was defined in simpler terms. Not to be overlooked is the well-known administrative fact that multiple solutions to a complex problem can make the problem less daunting and easier to handle.

QUESTIONING, CHALLENGING, AND ARGUING

Presidents who nurture the team's cognitive function purposefully strive to avoid oversimplifying problems that come before the team. They also try to avoid bringing premature closure to questions that need substantial thought and exploration. They urge their teams to raise sensitive questions, to challenge the status quo, and to argue points of inconsistency or contradiction.

One of the presidents participating in this study—a person who deliberately sought to strengthen his team's cognitive function—told us that he expects his group to "push me." Another said that he openly invites debates within the team in considering why "a chosen course of action may not be a prudent one." A third president told us that he sees a need to have group members "stand up to me and question my biases."

In teams where questions, challenges, and arguments such as these were possible, we learned from team members that, in their eyes, it was the president's style that made it all possible. In one such team, a member told us that the president "encourages interchange and disagreement and candor, . . . so much so that it would feel odd if we were not having arguments with him." Elaborating further, this member said: "I think most faculty would be surprised at how often the president is challenged in the cabinet. We take him on all the time. I think a president needs this kind of thing. The trust we have with him gives us the freedom to do this. When he is challenged, it forces him to reflect, and that has an impact."

Questioning, challenging and arguing occur more often when the president's relationship with the group is collegial. One president said, "I love it when people argue because I learn," but he was also sufficiently perceptive to realize that a norm of questioning and argument is not easy to come by, that it takes time to nurture as a way of team life. This president added, "Now that people are more familiar . . . they seem less afraid of me. . . . They will argue more, they are more inclined to question." At the beginning of a presidential term, people may not be fully attuned to such expectations. To challenge authority is, after all, antithetical to convention. One president's method of countering members' expectations was to choreograph "heated debates with team members until they came to realize that I wanted to see a problem from all angles" and "that it was all right to argue with the president."

MONITORING AND FEEDBACK

A presidential team can act as a monitoring and feedback mechanism in two ways: First, it may search for and attend to signs indicating that the institution is deviating from its desired course. One of the presidents participating in this study explained this process as "continually assessing" how well the "critical path we established for the college" is being followed. She also said that team members typically "keep their ear to the ground" in order to take "readings" of the state of the institution. Then periodically, she and others on the team "pause to reflect on these readings [to] gauge whether we are all functioning well [and to assess if] we are getting bogged down" in issues or details that might "make us lose sight of where the institution is headed."

Another way in which a presidential team can act as a monitoring and feedback system is by guarding the institution against pursuing outdated or no longer viable courses of action. For example, after commenting on how hard it can be to keep ideas going, a president explained that by challenging one another and by constantly stimulating the organization, the institution's top leadership group kept the college from becoming "entrenched, overly satisfied, and routinized."

For the team to be effective there has to be some tolerance for disorder on the part of the president as well as other team members. Teams that are truly effective (that think out loud, that challenge each other, and that argue among themselves) frequently consider new, unfamiliar, or unclear courses of action. They deviate often from what is comfortable and known to them. Presidents should bear in mind that creative problem solving is more likely to emerge from unstructured talks, which appear chaotic and wasteful to those who are impatient to get to the point, than from carefully ordered, formal agendas. The dialogues most conducive to successful monitoring and course adjustment are more likely to take place in informal settings that "allow the conversation to take the group" in unexpected directions and toward new or different understandings.

We should note, however, that in some institutions, unstructured discussion seldom takes place unless the president actively encourages group members to think and talk about "what [they] are hearing and seeing" rather than simply to deliver information in a utilitarian fashion. When the president demands information only, the group is likely to act only as a messenger. When the president asks the group to ponder what lies beneath the information that comes to the table, the group assumes the more complex role of information processor, sense maker, and information user and creator.

"Real" and "Illusory" Teams: How Presidents Use Their Teams

The three functions that teams may serve—utilitarian, expressive, and cognitive—are important in that together they respond to the diverse needs and expectations associated with collegiate operations. A president or other team builder who can conceive of all three functions, rather than being limited to just one, is in a position to mold a real team, one capable of meeting important administrative, human relations, and intellective issues. Real teams are complex because through their multiple functions they are able to address a diverse range of institutional issues.

Presidents with Real Teams

In our study, presidents with real teams tended to fit a consistent profile: First, when they described the nature of their teamwork, they presented their team as performing at least one useful activity in each of the three functional domains—the utilitarian, the expressive, and the cognitive. Second, virtually all the presidents with real teams cast their team's utilitarian function in terms of decision making and planning. Only one of the presidents with real teams was concerned about the team's information-delivery capacities. In sum, presidents with real teams thought of them in complex ways.

Presidents with Illusory Teams

Unlike the presidents with real teams, presidents with illusory teams utilized their groups only partially in that they focused on team functions in only one or two of the three domains presented in this chapter. For the most part, the illusory teams missed both the cognitive and expressive domains; they functioned at the most basic, utilitarian level of "doing," giving little attention to their processes of thinking and simply being together.

As we will note later, some of the presidents who openly stated a preference for what we call the illusory team, worried about the cacophony, confusion, and disorder that might ensue when multiple ideas move into motion, as they often do in the more complex, real teams. They seemed to distance themselves purposely from the idea of teamwork in its real form as we have presented it thus far. However, as we launched into interviews with these people, none of them stopped us with something like, "Your questions are irrelevant to me because I do not have a team." Rather, all but one of the eight presidents whose teams we deemed illusory told us that, in fact, they had teams. For these presidents, a cabinet composed of vice presidents was tantamount to a team, regardless of how limited that team's functions might be. Our observation was that these presidents' framework for thinking about teamwork was much narrower than the three-part framework that we discovered among the presidents engaged in real teamwork.

Presidents with illusory teams often told us that they felt more comfortable working with their administrative officers one to one—a sharp contrast to the group-oriented presidents with real teams. One president explained that he met only with "groups of two or three [because] when you get the five or six of us together it is not coherent." Another illusory team lacked the routines and symbols often associated with real teamwork, including regularly scheduled meetings.

In sum, presidents with illusory teams made use of their top administrative groups in limited, narrowly defined ways. The domains they bypassed most often were the expressive and the cognitive. They tended to describe their team's usefulness in terms of the utilitarian domain, particularly the team's ability to deliver information, rather than to think, question, challenge, or argue. Presidents with illusory teams were also concerned with exacting the loyalty of their administrators. They were not concerned with building a sense of closeness among team members. One president summed it up this way: "It is not that important to have scotch together on Friday afternoon. 'Living together' is not the issue." In contrast to this president's view, research suggests that effective groups typically balance solidarity, on the one hand, with task accomplishment on the other. Thus the time team members spend together over a drink on Fridays may be as important to the team's functioning as time spent getting things done (Goleman 1988) in a more utilitarian fashion. What stands out distinctively about the presidents with illusory teams is that they do not identify cognition as a useful team function.

A Once "Real" Team That Became "Illusory": The Case of Southern Plains College

The difference between real and illusory teamwork is stark when we watch a team change from one form to the other. A change such as this lets us see not only that people behave differently in the two models but also that their thinking and feeling differ. To illustrate just such a change, and to sharpen the contrast between real and illusory teamwork, we offer here the story of Southern Plains College (previously published in Bensimon 1990a).

Soon after taking office, the new president of Southern Plains let the "inherited" chief administrative officers know of his intention to discontinue the team approach to decision making to which they had become accustomed. Under the previous president the team had functioned like a "real" team. The chief administrators had been together for a long time and shared a strong sense of "groupness." The prevailing belief among all members of the group was that by acting as a cohesive body they had greater access to information and were more effective problem solvers than when they acted individually. For example, one said, "We used to look forward to cabinet meetings to find out about little things that can bite you if you are unaware of them." The cabinet meetings also provided a forum of interaction for busy administrators. One described it this way:

"I don't have time to find my colleagues to chitchat on a daily basis, so the meetings were good for that. We shared things, we passed information to one another, we questioned each other about small incidents." Essentially, these administrators were united in their faith that their manner of organizing and working "expanded their intelligence."

However, the group ceased to function as a real team. The processes that had contributed to making them a real team—a meeting held always on the same day and hour of every week, informal brainstorming as a problem-solving approach, sharing of information (including gossip and rumors) in an open manner, and consensual decision making—were suddenly replaced by a considerably more structured and formal process. The new president had learned and preferred to work with administrators individually and not as a group. The idea of a single conference table, with all the chief administrative officers getting involved in each other's domains, was quite outside his immediate experience. Before the new president took over, the administrative group's meetings had been organized around a loose and impromptu agenda, which allowed issues to be raised spontaneously. But to the new president, this approach seemed disorderly; it prompted conversations that were unfocused, making it appear that time was being wasted on seemingly irrelevant matters. These "problems" were addressed by the president's introduction of new processes: the agenda for the meeting was drawn up several days in advance, and each item was classified according to a predetermined category (information items, decision items, and so on).

The new structuring of the agenda elicited a new mode of interaction. Instead of engaging in prolonged debates and arguments as they had in the past, now each administrator gave a formal report on the status of her or his items. One administrator described the procedure as follows: "Now you are essentially making a presentation to the president, and your peers are your audience. Now you are looking for an okay from the president, where before we would all get involved in the discussion and in making the decision. But now, after you present the agenda item, you say, 'Mr. President, on the basis of what I have summed up, I'd like to recommend . . . ,' without the others chiming in." Another administrator summed up the effect of these changes by observing that suddenly "it felt like we were moving from family cooking to restaurant cooking."

While the newly imposed structure made it possible to deal more efficiently with single and unified problems, it could not accommodate issues that did not neatly fit into one of the prescribed agenda categories. To conform to the president's penchant for an orderly agenda, the chief administrators stopped bringing problems that were so abstract, complex, and value laden as to preclude quick and clean resolution. Unbeknownst to the president, who looked at the situation purely from his standpoint, efficiency was gained at the cost of the team's cognitive role, and what could have been a critical source of information and analysis for the newly installed president was shut off.

What is obvious about the change at Southern Plains College is that the team, as initially configured, featured a prominent expressive function. The team felt good together; members were comfortable with each other; they were completely open with each other. In this initial setting, the cognitive function also flourished. Members brainstormed together, offered insights, and tendered constructive criticism. This was a real team.

Under the new president, however, the more planned and organized agenda, rather than providing guidance and form, served to restrict conversation to all but the most utilitarian of activities (information giving, decision making). Moreover, the team's new internal process, which was highly formal and rational, served to constrain the type of personal and thinking-out-loud "chitchat" that characterized the team in its former existence, when thinking together and being together were more important than doing together.

What Gets in the Way? Conditions That Deter the Building of Real Teams

While in later chapters we discuss aspects of leadership and institutional life that are likely to facilitate the building of real teams, we consider here some of the barriers to real teamwork. What are the impediments to the building of teams that serve more than the utilitarian function, that provide emotional support, and that contribute cognitive effort? What stands in the way of the real team? As the case of Southern Plains College shows, the orientation of the team builder—in this case, the president—is a key factor in determining the real versus illusory character of the team.

The Team Builder's Leadership Orientation

The team builder may stand as a barrier to the full functioning of the team. The team builder's approach to teamwork may reflect, for example, the characteristics (including the limitations) of that person's approach to leadership generally. For example, some presidents (i.e., those designated as having illusory teams) may not use their teams for expressive or cognitive purposes because demanding loyalty and limiting access to information is consistent with their view of managerial success. They see the manager as the "guardian of the organization's knowledge base to heighten the importance of exclusivity" (Zuboff 1988, p. 238). Or, like the president of Southern Plains College, a team builder may be so concerned with orderliness and control as to openly impede expressive and cognitive activity among team members, at least during team meetings or at other official gatherings. At Southern Plains College the team conformed to the new, official team structure. However, the team members' informal exchanges and networking practices continued outside the rigid structure of the cabinet meetings and without the president's participation.

The converse is also true: Presidents and other administrators who use a democratic/political approach for institutional problem solving and goal-setting generally are likely to be effective in developing real teamwork (see Walker 1979). Leaders, and especially presidents, who tend toward a democratic/political style are likely to adhere to principles of administration based on open communication and free access to information, and they are likely to favor the use of negotiation, compromise, and persuasion in resolving problems; their approach to managing the larger organization is likely to parallel their approach to managing the work of their administrative teams. Moreover, leaders who use a democratic/political leadership style are particularly adept at developing real teams because they recognize that no one person is strong in all areas, because they are able to share and give credit to others, and because they recognize that conflict is a natural condition of human organization. We will discuss such aspects of team building again in chapter 6.

Institutional Context

Another factor that may affect real teamwork, particularly at the executive level, is institutional context. Our study shows that presidents in small institutions are more apt to have real teams. The opposite is true for presidents of large institutions, where we are likely to find very few real teams (Bensimon 1991b).

Contrary to what one might expect, our study suggests that as institutional size and complexity increase, real teams are likely to become more difficult to achieve. One explanation may be that characteristics of large and complex institutions, such as task specialization and loose coupling (Weick 1979), make them incompatible with real (and more tightly coupled) teamwork. Illusory teamwork may more closely match the organizational worlds of the large institutions. On the other hand, because smaller institutions are more tightly coupled, they may be more conducive settings for the tightly coupled real teams.

Specifically, we found that real teams are more likely to exist in small, private, four-year colleges than in large, public universities. This is consistent with the collegial governance model (Baldridge et al. 1978, Millett 1962, Rice & Austin 1988) typically attributed to small, private institutions. The absence of real teams in universities may be related to the strongly political nature of these institutions (Baldridge 1971), to their anarchic qualities (Cohen & March 1974), and to their tendencies to act like "adhocracies" (Weick 1983). Leadership in such institutions is likely to rely on power tactics, negotiation, coalitional dynamics, and persistence more than on collaboration. Again, what is true of the institution as a whole may be true also of the team.

This is not to say that real teams cannot exist in large universities. But it must be recognized that just as small colleges reflect characteristics that are conducive to real teamwork, universities possess characteristics (e.g., a high degree of differentiation among structural units, loose coupling) that are antithetical to real and complex teamwork. Consequently, university presidents who desire the benefits of teamwork that blends all three functions—cognitive, expressive, and utilitarian—must exert substantial effort to create a climate that supports it.

Our previous research (Neumann & Bensimon 1990) shows that university presidents are more likely to be externally focused than internally connected, for example, as they turn their attention to fundraising or to network building in the state and the nation. The typical university president has little time for the internal and rather contained activity of team building. Although teamwork was less evident at the executive level in universities, our research revealed that university presidents rely very heavily on their executive officers, using them, as one said, to "execute things because the president cannot do it all" and because they feel that they need to "resist getting dragged down to a level of inappropriate detail." University presidents described themselves as "aggressive at developing a formal reporting system" and as creating structures to alert them to problems "before they become full blown."

While university presidents appear to be particularly adept at using their teams for relatively utilitarian purposes (e.g., to "execute things because the president cannot do it all"), they may yet need to learn how to use their teams for reflective dialogue. A team may represent a time and place—an opportunity—to examine the meaning of issues and problems in light of the institution's mission, values, and aspirations. It may represent a setting within which meaning generally can be constructed. This, however, requires the team's ability to think together (the cognitive function) and also to support each other in their joint thinking (the expressive function).

Regardless of the president's position with regard to teams, the fact that teams do not typically exist at the upper reaches of university administration should not nullify the likelihood of their existence at middle or lower institutional levels. Because of the monumental complexity of university life, and because of the deep political rifts that often mark top-level university deliberations, these institutions may be able to support real teams and teamwork only at the level of the college or academic department. At this level, the turf battles (against opposing departments or colleges) characteristic of politically alive, loosely coupled systems, may actually inspire tight coupling within the academic unit—namely, the formation of teamlike structures. While we speculate that in the university teams are *not* absent but rather that they are situated differently than in small colleges, this is a question in need of further research.

Other Conditions That Affect Real Teamwork

A number of other conditions may affect the ability of a team to engage in real teamwork:

1. Whether or not the president feels at ease in sharing organizational leadership and decision making with the cabinet and whether or not the president wants to create a workplace that operates according to an egalitarian ethic are likely to affect the emergence or suppression of real teamwork (Lewis 1975 cited in Dyer 1987). Because the cognitive function requires exploration of areas beyond those that are known or seen as legitimate, it requires the ability to explore conceptions that range beyond the ordinary. This is likely to involve listening to voices that have not traditionally been at the center of the decision process rather than favoring conventional (and dominant) views.

2. Whether or not trust exists between the team builder and other team members and how comfortable all members feel in disclosing their vulnerabilities are also likely to affect the quality of teamwork. The expressive function is based on openness toward and trust in others. The cognitive function requires people to speak their thoughts openly—to risk being wrong and awkward—as the team searches for new ways to think about issues and problems. Without the openness and without the risk, a team is likely to withdraw into utilitarian behavior.

3. Whether or not there is a sense of respect for team members is also likely to affect the quality of teamwork. In the ideal team, meetings are taken seriously and are not canceled and rescheduled to fit the lead administrator's (or chairperson's) calendar. In one of our study institu-

tions, we heard this complaint: "We schedule to meet weekly, but that is often canceled because of the president's schedule. That is bad because it does not show respect for our time. The exceptions are too numerous." Complaints such as this were common on teams that we defined as primarily utilitarian and, therefore, illusory. They were not typically characteristic of real teams. In addition to the symbolic message of disrespect that this kind of schedule changing sends out to team members, there is also the more basic problem of substance. As a member of an illusory team noted, when the team fails to meet, it also "fail[s] to look at longer range issues, and [it] fail[s] to notice early warnings before a crisis hits." A brief qualification follows, however: some administrators may convene their teams too frequently, making members feel that they are at the beck and call of the lead administrator and that they must limit work outside the domain of the team. This kind of "over-meeting," with the schedule in the hands of the lead administrator, is as harmful as not meeting at all.

Summary

We have shown that presidential teams can function in diverse ways. They are likely to differ not only in terms of their utilitarian, expressive, and cognitive emphases but also in the amount of power they wield—in their potential effect on institutional life. Some teams, for example, may play strong and active leadership roles in their institutions. Others may play the roles of subordinate staff. Teams enjoy different degrees of influence. For example, teams with strong cognitive functions may exert significant leadership because they are actively involved in interpreting meaning. Cognitively oriented teams are in a position to shape, alter, and otherwise fashion the team builder's and other team members' understandings of a given situation, as well as the team's potential responses to that situation. This perspective differs radically from the conventional belief that the team builder (in many cases, the lead administrator) should shape the views of those who work with her or him.

We have also differentiated teams that are real—those that fulfill utilitarian, expressive, and cognitive functions—from those that are illusory—those focusing predominantly on the utilitarian function. In this study, the presidents who had real teams espoused a collectivist orientation to teamwork. They encouraged team members to think about global institutional issues rather than limiting them to specific domains of activity. They also described the team as an opportunity "to philosophize" jointly about institutional direction, and they frequently referred to their group's "ongoing conversations" and "shared sense of the institution."

In contrast, the presidents with illusory teams approached teamwork from an individualistic standpoint. They related to their administrators through formal (as opposed to personal) means. They were careful to maintain clear hierarchical distinctions between people in superior and subordinate roles. They used authoritarian language to emphasize the status difference between the president and the rest of the team. They restricted team members to specific institutional segments (e.g., academic affairs, budgetary matters) rather than acquainting them with the institution as a totality. Comments such as the following were quite common among this set of presidents:

I expect [the team] to carry out my orders.

They [team members] are more comfortable knowing the boundaries and who is God.

They carry forth to the campus my vision and goals.

They understand what I want to know and what I don't want to know.

Another difference between presidents with real teams and those with illusory teams is that the former tended to rely on the first-person plural ("we" and "us") in describing team actions, a verbal gesture that reinforced these presidents' collectivist orientation. In contrast, the presidents with illusory teams made more frequent use of the first-person singular pronoun ("I"), a gesture that defined them as separate, even remote, from the team. Presidents with illusory teams also tended toward paternalism more than did presidents with real teams. Their interviews were spiced with statements such as, "I make them [the team] believe I need them," or "I set an example for them, . . . I work hard so they will work hard." While some team builders may see the team as merely a utilitarian appendage to their own superordinate leadership, others see the very essence of leadership in the team rather than within themselves. Presidents in the team-building role who take the latter view—emphasizing the team rather than the self as leader—typically present themselves as their teams' care givers rather than as their heads.

Finally, in setting out the three functions of leadership teams we have tried to point out that there is more than just one way to be a team. Some teams fulfill only one basic function (utilitarian). Others, of a more complex variety, fulfill the basic function alongside other more sophisticated ones (cognitive and expressive). We turn now to what we deem the team's central task—thinking together. This is what separates an elemental, utilitarian team from a complex team engaged in sense making. It is also what separates the illusory from the real team.

4

Making Teams Work: The Art of Thinking Together

As we saw in the preceding chapter, the critical difference between real and illusory teams is the cognitive function. Illusory teams may be very active in accomplishing all manner of tasks, but they are generally weak as collective thinkers. For real teams, cognition is integral to teamwork. This chapter looks closely at the cognitive function—that is, team thinking, especially as it contrasts with team doing, and it gives particular attention to how team members may contribute as individuals to this important element of teamwork.

Teamwork as Thinking versus Doing

We often think of teams as vehicles of achievement and performance. That is, we judge a team's effectiveness by its abilities to accomplish expected ends (achievement) and by the strategies or techniques whereby team members strive for those ends (performance). Thus, we often think of teams in the active, visible sense as *doing* and *acting*, and we expect them to do and act particularly well in their own domain of interest and expertise.

What we often miss, however, is the fact that teams are involved in more than just *doing*—that the *doing* that we can see and account for is just the tip of the iceberg. Below the surface of a team's performance lie the more abstract activities of cognitive teamwork, including how team members perceive, discover, think, and create individually and interactively. In a sense, teamwork has two realities: There is the reality of performance, which is readily accessible to the interested and invited spectator. But there is also the reality of the team's internal contemplation, which is typically inaccessible to the spectator who is not a team participant. If we really want to understand how a team works, it is not enough to look at the team from the outside as an uninvolved spectator would, regardless of how carefully and comprehensively we track the details of the team's externally visible performance. To the extent that we can, we must enter the inside world of the team to examine the often confusing, disordered processes that a spectator, by virtue of not being involved, cannot see or hear, including team members' thinking, talking, wondering, asking, speculating, arguing, correcting, trying, rethinking, creating, trying again.

Analogies to fields outside higher education leadership are instructive. Most people in our culture enjoy spectator activities involving "teams," defined in the broadest sense as purposeful, coordinated groups with aims of performance. We refer here not only to team performances such as football and basketball games, but to other teamlike performances, including dance (a dance troupe may be viewed as a team), movies and plays (a dramatic production company, including cast and crew, also fits our definition of *team*), and concerts (both a wind ensemble and a rock band are performance teams). In going to a football game, we hope to see our team score high points as players run through carefully strategized maneuvers. In attending a ballet, a movie, a play, or a concert, we hope to encounter artistry at its best, or at least to get some decent entertainment.

While athletic teams, dance troupes, production companies, and musical ensembles differ from college and university leadership teams—and from each other—in important ways (e.g., in the "team" leader's directiveness, in group members' prerogative to initiate and reinterpret, in the presence or absence of a script), they help make the point about the cognitive dimensions of teamwork. As spectators, we attend to the final productions of these various "teams"—the execution of the athletic team's field plays, the style and technique of the dancers' movements, the authenticity of the actors' dramatization, the crafting of the musicians' performance. Yet in attending to performances or final productions such as these, we often miss the "inside stories" of the actual performing and producing. For example, we don't know what the quarterback is thinking as he scans the field, or what the musician is contemplating as she looks intently at her music. While we see and hear what both eventually *do* as part of their performance, we have no access to their thinking *before* they do it and *as* they do it. Similarly, we have little access to the thinking and creating that occurred for weeks, months, and years prior to each of these performances—for example, as coaches and athletes designed their plays, as dancers choreographed their steps, as directors and actors adjusted stage presentation, and as musicians learned to play together. And yet, to appreciate the quality of each of these teams' performances, we need to understand this kind of less visible, cognitive work occurring behind the scenes of the performance itself and guiding it. Moreover, if we really wanted to *learn* something about how to play football well as a team, or how to produce a play as a teamlike cast and crew, it would not be enough to watch the external motions of these teams at work. We would need to tap into the interactive thinking behind the motion as well.

We can consider the performance of college and university leadership teams in a similar way. When we observe leadership teams at work we are, in effect, tuning into their performance, although the performance of a president's or dean's team is not likely to be as staged, or as entertaining, as our previous examples. For example, we notice the regularity of team meetings, the content and frequency of telephone conversations, the quantity of paper flows between individuals' offices, the formal and informal character of conversation among team members. We also tune into the achievements of leadership teams, whether in the form of plans, decisions, or budgets. Yet what we often miss, in analyzing the teamwork of persons in institutional leadership roles, is the inside story of the team—the processes of discovering, thinking, shaping, and creating that make up the more private, internal, contemplative choreography of teamwork: What makes a leadership team pursue a particular agenda? Why do team members give one topic more attention than others? How do team members work together in shaping the agenda? To what extent do they transform existent agendas, and how? To what extent do team members think together, and how? What does it mean to think as a team, and how can a team improve its collective thinking?

In this chapter we consider the thinking side of teamwork—the side that can't be seen because it occurs usually behind closed doors, invisible to the public eye. We believe that in teams that think together, whether in full view of their organizational audience or in the privacy of their meeting room, the cognitive and utilitarian functions combine, each informing the other. What results is a team engaged in active reflection and simultaneously in reflective action. We will return to this point later.

Team Thinking

We have probably learned more about the cognitive and interactive dimensions of executive decision making from the Cuban missile crisis than from any other event in recorded history. Not only did that event grip the attention of scholars concerned with Cuban culture and history,

American-Soviet relations, and modern warfare, it also captivated analysts concerned with how people make decisions, particularly momentous
decisions—including the psychological and sociological factors that influence what they see, know, and believe. In his book, *Essence of Decision:
Explaining the Cuban Missile Crisis*, Graham T. Allison (1971) sets out
three very different frames for explaining the conditions and events of
the crisis. Each yields a different interpretation of what happened and
why during those difficult and frightening weeks in 1962. What Allison's
book brings out is the fact that different people make sense of the same
reality in different ways, and that a complete interpretation of what is
really happening is likely to combine facets of multiple frames rather
than adopting one view to the exclusion of others.

In his well-known analyses of several major policy blunders, including
the Bay of Pigs, the Korean conflict, and the escalation of the Vietnam
War, Irving L. Janis (1972) drives this message home even more firmly
by pointing out how dangerous it can be for leaders to assume their
team's unanimity on an issue, and thereby to attend to just one interpretation of the team's reality while excluding competing, and potentially
insightful perspectives. In brief, Janis's study emphasizes the hazards of
"groupthink," a phenomenon whereby people working in groups ignore
their individual thinking (even their individual consciences) in favor of
going along with the dominant group view. Individual beliefs, concerns,
criticisms, and understandings of whatever is being talked about are
pushed under the surface so that a unanimous voice of the group can
emerge. As we noted in chapter 1, groupthink is one of the potential
disadvantages, even hazards, of teamwork.

Through our research we have come to differentiate Janis's concept of
"groupthink" from the concept of "team thinking." While groupthink
involves the suppression of individual thought and voice, team thinking
requires individuals to work their minds and express their thinking publicly, to other team members, regardless of how divergent from the group
norm their thinking may be and regardless of the topic under discussion.
Team thinking *assumes* that individuals see the world differently, that
they process information differently, that they make sense of life in organizations (and outside them) differently. It also requires team members
to develop their own unique thinking capacities and to exercise them
openly, actively, and freely.

The other side of the coin applies as well. Team thinking requires that,
in addition to exercising their individual thinking abilities, the members
of a team must be open to the *different* thinking processes of other
members of the team. They must be tolerant of different thinking

approaches and different ways of making sense, even if what they hear from their teammates is at great odds with their own conceptions of the world. Thus team thinking requires that team members assert their own views and their own ways of thinking (in as understandable a way as possible), but it also requires that they listen to their colleagues on the team—and that they develop the skills to really *hear* divergent ways of making sense of a common organizational world.

How Does Team Thinking Work?

Team thinking begins with the different contributions of individual members of the team to the team's collective knowing—the team's collective understanding of whatever issues are before it. What kinds of different thinking processes or styles might individual team members bring to—or induce within—their group?

In analyzing the college and university administrative teams participating in this study, Anna Neumann (1991c) responded to this question by describing eight thinking roles that college administrators often play on the president's top leadership team.* Using methods of qualitative analysis to search for patterns of diversity within teams and across teams, Neumann examined team members' images of their own and each other's contributions to their teams, including their statements about roles they wished their team had but believed it missed. The result resembled a series of team "scripts," some of which were rich in roles while others were more sparse, sounding more like monologues. The following section describes the eight thinking roles emerging from Neumann's study. Table 4.1 presents them also in summary form. The chapter concludes with an illustration of how these roles and the team processes they instigated played out in a real situation taken from our research sample, along with recommendations for cultivation of the roles in the context of a leadership team. While the eight roles were based on data derived only through interviews with the members of presidential teams, we believe that they can be helpful to people seeking to understand other types of teams as well—for example, administrative teams at the dean's level or within a vice presidential division, teamlike committees in academic departments, business office staffs, work groups in student affairs divisions, and so forth.

*The following discussion elaborates on a research report by Anna Neumann titled "The Thinking Team: Toward a Cognitive Model of Administrative Teamwork in Higher Education," *Journal of Higher Education* 62, no. 5 (September/October 1991), 485–513.

Table 4.1
Eight Thinking Roles for a Presidential Team

Roles in the "core" of team thinking:

Definer:	Voices a view of the team's reality and thereby creates that reality
Analyst:	Provides a deep examination of issues previously defined (e.g., by assessing components of a problem)
Interpreter:	Translates how people outside the team are likely to see and understand issues at hand
Critic:	Offers redefinition, reanalysis, or reinterpretation of issues before the team
Synthesizer:	Elicits diverse thinking roles and facilitates the construction of a summative team reality

Roles that support the "core":

Disparity Monitor:	Assesses how people outside the team in fact make sense of the team's actions
Task Monitor:	Strives to remove obstacles to team thinking, facilitates the team's work processes in general
Emotional Monitor:	Helps to establish and maintain the human, personal, and emotional context within which team thinking occurs

Eight Thinking Roles

A "thinking role" refers to a certain form of thinking yielding a specific kind of result (Neumann 1991c). What is particularly important about the idea of a thinking role is that it implies that thinking is not just one hard and fast process. Rather, thinking is a conglomerate verb, referring to a wide variety of mental processes (e.g., defining, analyzing, synthesizing), each yielding different kinds of mental results (e.g., a definition or declaration of a new problem, the analysis of the problem, the synthesizing of abundant information concerning the problem). A thinking role refers to the playing out of one specific type of thinking (e.g., the role of analyzing) with one specific type of result (e.g., analysis). A single leadership team may therefore reflect several different thinking roles. As we note later, a team may reflect very few thinking roles as well. Roles and people, however, are not the same thing, and any individual may play any number of roles or no roles.

But what exactly does it mean to play a particular thinking role? The answer to this question is very important because this is what differentiates the leadership team with a prominent cognitive function from the athletic team and also from the leadership team that shows only a utilitarian function. In addition to carrying out a particular form of thinking, the idea of "playing a role" commonly refers to *the initiating of a team process that encompasses all (or most) other team players.* Thus a person in the team role of "analyst" does much more than analyze situations. In offering an initial analysis, she or he draws the whole team into a collective process of analysis that continues until another player initiates a different team process (e.g., critique) by enacting a different role (i.e., the critic role).

The Core of Team Thinking

The first five roles (Definer, Analyst, Interpreter, Critic, and Synthesizer) represent the core of team thinking. Collectively, these five interact in selecting, creating, elaborating, and shaping the issues the team attends to. The last three roles (Disparity Monitor, Task Monitor, Emotional Monitor) support, facilitate, maintain, and redirect the work of this core.

THE DEFINER

The team's Definer gives voice to her view of the team's reality, thereby stimulating a team process of reality definition. This is how team and institutional agendas are often created. In presenting what she sees "out there," the Definer outlines the team's formal and informal agenda, declaring that the team should put its collective mind to a certain topic (and thereby ignore or sidestep other potential topics).

Is the person in the Definer role simply smarter than other members of the team, for example, seeing problems on the horizon that others on the team may not? Our research suggests that most Definers do not just "discover" things "out there" that are hidden to others. Rather, like artists, they themselves often invent designs within reality.

Our study, like many others (Berger & Luckmann 1966, Pettigrew 1979, Weick 1979), suggests that the social life that we share with others (for example, life in a college) is something that we fashion, at least in part, through our own thinking and our own ways of knowing. We view life in organizations not as predefined according to a given order that everyone understands in exactly the same way but rather as a haphazard, unending array of thoughts and behaviors, issues and problems, sights and sounds. Life in organizations (and colleges are no exception) is something of a gigantic stream of activity that we enter, individually and collectively (Cohen & March 1974, Birnbaum 1988), and we try to make some sense out of that corner of the stream in which we physically find

ourselves. In making sense we enact behaviors that add to the already
burgeoning activity around us, leaving it to others to sort out what our
small additions mean (Weick 1979). Our human limitations prevent us
from working with more than the details of our small corner of the
stream. And even in our small corner, different individuals may bring
different interpretations to what lies there and how it might be arranged.

What does the general disorder of organizations have to do with the
Definer role on the team? The Definer is quick to try to bring some sense
to how the pieces of her part of the stream fall together. And she guesses
how others, in other parts of the stream, will make sense of what they
see in such a way that it will affect the work of the team. What is important
to realize is that one person's "defining" may be quite different from
another person's "defining" and that neither may be right or wrong
because, beneath their orderly definitions, there is no fundamental, ultimately true order. There is simply the stream. Unfortunately, the tendency
to interpret organizational realities in diverse ways often leads to misunderstanding and conflict, particularly when people fail to realize that
while they may use the same words to describe what they think is happening, they may actually mean very different things (Neumann 1991b).

Leadership, as we view it, involves bringing a comfortable, meaningful
sense of order to portions of the stream, getting others to see that order
and believe in it, getting others to hold onto it (because in doing so, they
create it for themselves), regardless of whether or not they see the chaotic
stream that lies below. The team's Definers contribute to leadership by
sketching out their own views of meaning within the stream. They are
guided in this meaning-making task by their deepest values, personal
understandings, and beliefs about the nature of people and the world.

One of the key questions that we face in teams and in organizations
generally is who is it that we permit to do our defining, and whom do
we position to spur or direct our collective thinking? Whose voices do
we listen to? Whose views do we struggle to understand and accept,
regardless of how different they may be from our own? Why do we allow
some people to step into the Definer role freely but not others?

The temptation on many teams and in many colleges is simply to let
the person in the highest formal position (e.g., the president) do the
defining. But there are likely to be other dynamics at play as well: On
many teams the Definer role goes easily to a person who reflects the
social majority on the team, most often a group of white males, often
with strong roots in the local culture. However, some of the strongest
teams that we have seen try consciously to spread the Definer role around,
for example, by attending to "marginal" voices both on and off the team:
vice presidents and faculty members (as opposed to the president or

trustees), women (versus men) and ethnic minorities (rather than whites), strangers to the college and the region (as opposed to long-time residents), and persons who are young and new to their profession (rather than seasoned).

While we view the inclusion of marginal voices within the team— particularly in the role of Definer—as crucial, we must add an important qualification. Occasionally a team turns to the solo woman or solo ethnic minority member on the team to act as a Definer, but only with regard to women's issues or minority issues. While some teams might view this as a positive step (who could speak better for women than a woman?), it falls short in two ways: First, the solo woman or minority person who is cast as the team's expert on women's or minority issues may, by virtue of identification with a restricted agenda, be blocked from acting as a Definer on larger issues. Second, a team that divides its labor so that only one person is responsible for attending to the concerns of women or ethnic minorities may give out the message to other team members that they need not be vigilant on these issues because someone else is "covering that base." A team that subjects the Defining role to just such a division of labor creates, in effect, an illusory Definer. Authentic defining requires the freedom of all team members to choose, shape, and create topics within any and all domains.

THE ANALYST

Given an issue or problem that the team's Definer has framed for the group's attention, the Analyst examines it, taking it apart, viewing it from diverse angles, studying it against larger contexts, assessing its source and pattern of development, and projecting its effects or exploring its ramifications in diverse scenarios. By initiating this kind of examination, the Analyst prompts others to respond to his view—for example, by supporting, questioning, exploring, extending, or rebutting it.

In one institution participating in our study, the president's leadership team was faced with the question of whether to buy an extremely expensive classic pipe organ for the college's new chapel auditorium or a less expensive electronic organ. The faculty committee charged with investigating the question recommended the more expensive option, giving, as one interviewee told us, the preferred "manufacturer and even the style." While the president's initial reaction was to go with the committee's choice because of the organ's symbolic value to the institution, several Analysts on the team voiced their reservations, noting both the question of time ("It will take six years to get it in") and, more important, the cost relative to other campus needs ("We asked them [the recommending committee] to justify the acquisition in terms of the academic program"). A team member who appeared particularly expert in the Analyst role elaborated:

> Can we in good conscience ask for this organ if we are trying to teach without adequate facilities in other areas—for example, without a stage for the Theater Arts Department?. . . My frustration in this is that I have running through my head everything else that we need. The Life Sciences Department wants a new building, and they [like the people who want the pipe organ] want to have the best. . . . Everyone wants a Cadillac, and we are a Chevrolet institution. So if we get the pipe organ, how can we be fair to the rest of the campus population?

The Analyst role differs from the Definer role in this way: If we compare the Definer to an artist sketching designs of the reality she sees around her, then the Analyst is the observer who peers deeply into that picture in an effort to comprehend it. The Analyst usually examines the Definer's picture from the inside—for example, in terms of its component parts and their interrelationships. However, he also considers the patterns that might emerge when the picture is viewed from different angles or against different backgrounds.

While the Definer originates an issue (or design within reality) by declaring, "This is what we have," the Analyst responds by probing, "What do we, in fact, have here?" He then takes the issue apart, holds it up, or turns it over in an effort to find out. While he may examine the internal composition of the Definer's presentation of reality (even critiquing it), he does not question the definitional frame in which it is cast, nor does he consider alternative frames. The team process that the Analyst engenders respects the same limits.

THE INTERPRETER

The Interpreter also takes, as her point of departure, the Definer's view of reality. She does not question its goodness or authority. She merely explains to the Definer and others on the team how other people, outside the team, will see and understand whatever issue is at hand. Unlike the Analyst, the Interpreter rarely looks inside an issue or problem (i.e., taking it apart to understand its internal dynamics), but rather she serves as something of a translator, comparing the Definer's image of whatever issue is at hand to the image that is likely to crop up in the minds of the faculty, students, or college community generally. If the Definer's portrayal of reality is viewed as a picture, then the Interpreter initiates a process whereby the team, as a whole, considers what other outside viewers will make of it.

The person who assumes the Interpreter role is likely to have extensive experience with a particular college constituency—for example, the faculty, trustees, community, students, or parents. She will know that constituency so well that she will be able to guess what they will see and how they will make sense of a particular event or team action. One of the biggest mistakes that administrators make is to believe that what they see and believe is shared exactly by others around them—in short, that all people see the same things and make the same sense out of what they see. New college presidents, in particular, may fail to realize that the things that mattered most to faculty and others in their former institutions may not matter at all in their new contexts, and vice versa (Neumann 1990a). And on first entering their new institutions, they may neglect to devote time to identifying what people consider to be important in their settings and also to determining what is of lesser consequence to them (Bensimon 1990a). The Interpreters on the team can help the president with these tasks.

We have spoken with presidents who attributed their biggest mistakes to taking action in light of what they had learned about good administrative practice in other institutions. For example, one president made major changes in search procedures for top-level administrators without consulting the faculty; he could have done this in his previous position, but in his new college, he elicited faculty resentment. And another new president took a personnel action against a faculty member, as he could easily have done in his former institution, but this resulted in a major and long-term confrontation with the faculty in the new institution. In both cases the president did what he believed to be acceptable on the basis of his former experience. He did not pause long enough to elicit other people's interpretations of how the faculty would see and understand his action. In both cases, the president could have used a team colleague capable of filling the Interpreter role and would have benefitted from a team process that supported interpretation.

THE CRITIC

While the Analyst and Interpreter typically work off the Definer's agenda—exploring it item by item, pointing out its weaknesses and strengths, interpreting its unique meanings for others—the Critic is likely to propose a fundamentally different point of departure for the group. He may offer a redefinition of the agenda to which the team should attend (by altering the issues to which the team attends), a reanalysis of one or more issues currently being considered by the team (by offering a different frame of analysis), or a reinterpretation of the meaning of an issue at hand (by bringing in a different constituency's point of view and arguing for its due consideration).

The Critic often tends to rub against the grain: He may argue against the team's current agenda, thus countering the views of Definers. He may question the team's favored analytic approach, thereby clashing with an Analyst. He may show little concern for the likely reactions of a particular constituency, running headlong into the Interpreter. While in some cases the Critic may inspire a teamwide process of critique, he often has to take a stand alone or with little immediate support.

Critics may raise their questions for diverse reasons. Politically, they may wish to address one particular agenda rather than another. Intellectually, they may be bored or frustrated with business-as-usual or with thinking-as-usual, preferring instead to find a different view, a different understanding, and a different experience. Morally, they may sense that what the team is doing (or what it is neglecting to do) is hurting someone whose presence is not visible or understandable to the team, and they may begin to pave the ground for reforms in who the team listens to, how it thinks, what it knows, and how it acts. The Critic raises issues that others may take for granted or prefer not to acknowledge. The Critic also encourages the team to recognize the differences, rifts, and oppositions that are nearly always embedded in myths of consensus—differences that some people would prefer not to see.

Given the Critic's often divergent and oppositional point of view, he may be admired or disdained by his team colleagues. Some teams see their Critics as providing "a breath of fresh air." Others see them merely as "keeping things stirred up." Still others describe the Critic as "going too far, . . . irritating the others too much" and as engendering "divisiveness" on the team. Teams vary in how much they appreciate the Critic role, and people in the Critic role vary in how they enact it and also in their abilities to encourage others to join in a team process of critique.

THE SYNTHESIZER

The team's Synthesizer listens to and participates in the deliberative processes instigated by the team's Definers, Analysts, Interpreters, and Critics and builds from them a summative picture, which she articulates as the team's reality. While the Synthesizer and Definer roles may be played by one person, they remain two distinct roles. There are important differences between them: The Definer presents a raw conception of an issue or problem, a conceptual sketch with little body, weight, or meaning. The Definer's image is often minimalist in its presentation and ungrounded in its form. In contrast, the Synthesizer's conception of the same issue is usually a rich, expansive, and detailed picture crafted through the team's analysis, interpretation, and critique. While in some instances the "synthesis" may resemble the initial "definition," it may also differ radically from it. Those who engage in defining typically sketch images. Those who engage in synthesis listen to and orchestrate the voices of others on the team who, through their skills in definition, analysis, interpretation, and critique, may flesh out—or totally redraw—the original design.

The job of team orchestration has many parts. In some teams, the Synthesizer is known to "ask the right questions . . . [to] stimulate our [team members'] thinking." Thus she encourages and elicits individual contributions to team issues, for example, by "providing an atmosphere for candid interchange" among team members. In line with this task, the Synthesizer opens herself "to learning from them" so as to "see more than what each of them sees individually" and to "bring divergent views together." Finally, the Synthesizer acknowledges those moments in a team's life when, no matter how good the team's thinking is, the ambiguity surrounding a problem prevents understanding. At these times, the Synthesizer points out to the team that, despite the confusion and gaps, they must move on.

To summarize, the role of the Synthesizer is to engage team members in thinking, as each knows best how to do, about issues that the Definer initially points out, to learn from each of them, to help them learn from each other, and to help the group bring its divergent understandings together.

Supporting the Core of Team Thinking

Rather than contributing directly to the *substance* of team thinking, as the five roles defined above do, the remaining three roles shape the condition of the team's thinking by monitoring how people outside the team view team members' behaviors, by facilitating the direction and pace with which the team's thinking proceeds, and by responding to the feelings of individual team members as they engage in their collective cognitive work.

THE DISPARITY MONITOR

The Disparity Monitor and the Interpreter represent similar roles in that both provide the team with information on what persons outside the team think of the actions that the team is taking (or neglecting to take). However, there is a very important difference between the two.

The Interpreter helps the team work through scenarios of potential action—what the team *might* do, what actions the team *might* take. She predicts how people outside the team will see a particular team action. Thus the Interpreter focuses on the future—on what will happen *if* the team does something in particular. In this sense, the Interpreter is part of the team's *creating* core.

The Disparity Monitor, on the other hand, steps in once the team moves into action—once it undertakes its agenda actively. The team has little need for predictions at this point. Rather, what the team needs now is someone to watch, listen, and otherwise monitor how people outside the team do *in fact* make sense of the team's actions—what people outside see, what they say, and how they feel about whatever the team is doing.

The Disparity Monitor usually taps the views of faculty, students, community members, trustees, and others informally—for example, in the lunchroom, over coffee, in hallways. This role is rarely played through formal survey or interview procedures; it works primarily through more personal, word-of-mouth communication.

A Disparity Monitor is good with people, has usually been around the institution long enough to have the ear and confidence of a particular constituency, probes gently but efficiently about people's views, and knows how to listen extremely well. The person in the Disparity Monitor role, like the Interpreter, may have once been a member of the constituency to which he listens, in which case he usually achieved a respected senior role within its ranks (e.g., the faculty elder). But what is particularly important is that the person in the Disparity Monitor role *continues* as a member of that constituency (e.g., the faculty) even though he now holds membership as well within a very different constituency (e.g., top-level administration). This double membership is often very difficult, especially when the Disparity Monitor, by virtue of mixed affiliations, must cross between traditionally separate bureaucratic (e.g., administration) and professional (e.g., faculty) terrains.

Our study suggests that experienced presidents and new presidents use the Disparity Monitor in different ways. New presidents, for example, are often much concerned about what their actions look like to their institutions and whether people are happy with what the president or the team is doing. The new president typically goes out of the way either to serve as the team's Disparity Monitor himself by asking people informally what they think of certain activities or, more commonly, to encourage members of the team to do so. On some teams, new presidents may virtually go too far in seeking out other people's views, hinging their every action on what they think they look like to others on the outside. In such teams, the Disparity Monitor plays an overwhelming role, at times directing the team.

The opposite phenomenon seems to occur among more experienced presidents. Once they are established in office and comfortable with their knowledge of the institution and what people think of them, presidents may begin to make less use of the Disparity Monitor role. The president and others on the team may think they know how the institution is responding to whatever the team is doing, and they may feel so confident about this that they do not check out their expectations through the "testing" that the Disparity Monitor typically provides. In this kind of situation, the president, and the team, may over time lose touch with the rest of the institution.

THE TASK MONITOR

The Task Monitor, like the Definer, is concerned with the team's agenda, but in different ways. As described earlier, the role of the Definer is to initiate—to outline and give original form to—the issues to which the team eventually attends. In short, the Definer "puts the issues on the table" for the team. Unlike the Critic, the Task Monitor does not question the suitability of these issues, nor does she present alternatives. Rather, like the Analyst and Interpreter, the Task Monitor works with what the Definer has given her. However, while the Analyst and Interpreter work with the actual content or substance of the Definer's issues (looking more closely within them, translating what they are likely to mean to others), the Task Monitor pays particular attention to the group's work processes.

The Task Monitor is something of a team manager for some leadership groups, helping the team to order its priorities and actions, reminding team members of their aims, and checking frequently that key tasks are being accomplished. For others she is an all-around assistant, making herself available to pick up the loose ends of projects that no one else can or will pick up. For still others she is a referral agent, for example, reminding a team member faced with an exceptionally challenging problem that someone else in the institution faced a similar problem in the past and suggesting that the team member consult that person for insights or advice. The point is that the role of the Task Monitor is to remove whatever obstacles may be in the way of getting the job of team thinking done and to facilitate the processes of work.

On many teams, the managerial facet of the Task Monitor role involves asking, What do we want to achieve? and then reminding team members of this goal on a regular basis. As a manager, the Task Monitor also considers the steps that the team is taking at any given moment, and she often wonders out loud how a particular action (or set of actions) is contributing to the team's desired goals. While this managerial dimension of the Task Monitor role may sound particularly linear, it need not be. In fact, a tendency toward overlinearity on the part of the Task Monitor can be quite harmful to good teamwork. Some Task Monitors, for example, are well aware that the work of leadership is not and cannot be purely logical or even fully thought out, and that it is quite hard for teams to think first, act second, evaluate third, and so on, in a standard, rational decision-making mode. Sometimes teams (and individuals) simply take action—without knowing what they are doing or why they are doing it—and make sense of what they do *after* they do it, or they realize what they are doing *as* they do it (see Weick 1979 and Schon 1983).

In this kind of situation, a Task Monitor who is overly rigid and rational, wanting to know how every step fits into a final grand plan, would be a detriment to the work of the team. On the other hand, a Task Monitor who understands that sometimes people act and then think—or that their acting spurs their thinking—rather than the conventional reverse, will be wise enough to let this kind of creative teamplay work itself out. Nonetheless, the Task Monitor remains sensitive to the issue of "calling time" when jobs simply need to get done or decisions made.

THE EMOTIONAL MONITOR

The Emotional Monitor serves as a reminder that the thinking that is at the center of much teamwork is closely related to human feeling and emotion. The thinkers are human, and they may have strong feelings about the work they are doing, about the intensity of their interactive thinking, about their teammates' views and contributions in relation to their own, and about the positions that they may find themselves in. The Emotional Monitor serves as a reminder that it is impossible for team members to think continuously or unfeelingly, as though they were machines, and that it is very important to examine how people feel about the content and process of their work together.

The Emotional Monitor may contribute to team thinking in diverse ways. For example, a team that finds itself in a nonstop race against deadlines as members work together on multiple fronts may benefit from the Emotional Monitor who suddenly looks at and comments on their substantive concerns from a comical angle. Even a brief diversion that cuts momentarily through the organizational drama may allow some stress release, or at least enough of a stepping away from the work at hand to lend some perspective. The Emotional Monitor also serves as a reminder that despite the seriousness of the team's work, it ought to be enjoyable and that occasionally, maybe even frequently, it can be fun. The Emotional Monitor can put people back in touch with what is particularly meaningful, pleasant, or important in their work. The person in an Emotional Monitoring role may speak to the group as a whole, reminding them that it is important to look away, at least briefly, from the seriousness of their work. Or he may speak individually to team members about what they are feeling. He may also point out to team members how they are making others feel. The Emotional Monitor is both a supporter and a cheerleader—one who listens, empathizes, and encourages, and one who reminds and urges others to do the same.

Because team thinking is interactive work, the quality of personal interactions and relationships is of central concern. It is very hard for people who dislike each other or misunderstand each other to work together. The Emotional Monitor is particularly sensitive to relational issues such as these, monitoring and responding to them as they emerge. While some personal conflicts are beyond the capacity of any individual to handle, some may be caught just as they surface, and in this way, working relationships and friendships may be salvaged. In addition to dealing with conflictual relationships, the Emotional Monitor is also concerned with newly developing relationships. As new members join a long-time team, they search for ways to fit, and they often risk being excluded. The person in an Emotional Monitoring role often makes it his business to translate the team's dynamics to a new member, to get to know this individual, and to translate the new member's views to other team members.

In sum, the Emotional Monitor helps establish and hold together the human context of the team's thinking and of its work generally.

Team Thinking: A Collective View

When we put these various thinking roles together, we create something of a thinking system: The Definer initiates the team's defining process—that is, the selection, or invention, of its agenda, the topics to which it will devote its attention and energies. The Analyst and the Interpreter spur the processing of these issues. The Critic introduces a reexamination of what has already been defined, analyzed, and interpreted—for example, proposing alternative issues, viewpoints, or translations. The Synthesizer stimulates the orchestration of this thinking core, for example, by creating an environment that allows team members to bring forth their best talents, by learning from each member, and by forging an enlarged understanding of the issues at hand from diverse contributions. The Disparity Monitor, by informing the team of what people on the outside see, the Task Monitor, by keeping the team on course, and the Emotional Monitor, by urging the team to attend to the emotional side of teamwork or to break momentarily from its seriousness, support and otherwise facilitate the work of team thinking. Viewed this way, a team is anything but an instrument. Rather, it resembles a complex and connected social brain at work. It is through these roles and processes that the team's critical cognitive function converts a purely utilitarian group into a complex team that thinks as it acts. The enactment of the thinking roles converts teamwork from illusion into reality.

Who Plays Which Role?

Several things should be remembered about these various roles. First, as we have noted already, persons in the thinking roles, and especially in the core roles of Definer, Analyst, Interpreter, Critic, and Synthesizer, may themselves engage in role-specific activity (e.g., defining, analyzing, and so forth), but in doing so, they *also* enact a group process of joint definition, analysis, interpretation, critique, or synthesis that draws in most, or at least some, of the others on the team. Thus we can think of a role, especially a "core" role, as enacting a group process as much as we can think of it as performing or accomplishing a specific, self-contained activity.

Second, thinking roles (e.g., Definer, Analyst, and so forth) are totally separate and different from operational roles (e.g., president, academic VP, business VP). For example, a college president need not always act in the Definer role within her team (although our data suggest that most presidents do, in fact, play that role at one time or another). Also a person's area of responsibility (e.g., financial affairs, student affairs, academic affairs) need not correlate neatly with his thinking role. A person with the operational responsibilities of vice president for business affairs is as likely to be an Emotional Monitor as an Analyst on the college's top administrative team. A vice president for student affairs is as likely to be a Definer or Task Monitor as an Interpreter or Emotional Monitor. In sum, any one person on the team might play any one of the thinking roles. There are no clear-cut restrictions.

Third, any one person on the team might play several roles. Thus one person might be both an Emotional Monitor and a Synthesizer. And another could be an Interpreter, Disparity Monitor, and Task Monitor.

Fourth, any of the thinking roles might be played by any number of persons on the team. Thus, it is possible for a team to have three or four people in the Interpreter role, five or more in the Definer role, and so forth, with different individuals assuming different roles for different issues at different times.

Fifth, while some teams may have all (or most) of the roles, others may have very few. Those with few thinking roles, especially in the core, are likely to represent *illusions* of teamwork in that they focus mostly on the utilitarian dimension of the team process (i.e., getting things done) while excluding the cognitive.

Conflict and Tension among Thinking Roles

Having a team Critic, Definer, Interpreter, or any of the other roles is not always a sign that a team is working productively or harmoniously. Different ways of thinking may breed conflicts of understanding. And while a person in a certain role (e.g., the Interpreter) may try to stimulate a certain group process (e.g., interpretation), she may be unsuccessful for a variety of reasons. Consider the following examples: While the Critic may introduce a new and creative point of view, he may have an abrasive style, or he may come up with ideas that are not applicable to his particular context. As a result, others on the team may prefer not to take up his point. A Definer may provide the team with a useful agenda, but persons in this role can be overbearing, insisting on their definitions of their team's realities at the expense of others' views. In preventing others from sharing the Definer role, a Definer may in effect suppress a teamwide defining process. An Interpreter may play an important role in describing how various college constituencies will see the team's actions, but at the same time the Interpreter may resist the findings of Disparity Monitors who tap what is actually occurring outside or the ideas of Critics who prefer to depart from an Interpreter's more traditional understandings.

Above all, team thinking requires openness to the viewpoints of others. It also requires an ability to articulate clearly one's own point of view and to assess others' understanding of it. Finally, team thinking requires a desire, among all team members, to synthesize or orchestrate for openness and balance, rather than for single-sided dominance. We return to this point later in this chapter, but first we present the eight thinking roles as we found them in "live" form at one of the colleges participating in the study. The top administrators of Silver College compose a real, cognitively oriented team with all eight roles at work.

Team Thinking at Silver College

Silver College is a pseudonym for one of the institutions participating in our research on presidential leadership teams in higher education. The president, Margaret Book, was relatively new to the college and to the presidential role. However, in less than four years in office, she succeeded in turning the seriously declining college around. In 1989, the college, bereft of financial reserves, continued to face a shaky financial future, but the serious and steady decline that disfigured the college in past years had stopped.

During Margaret Book's term of office, Silver's enrollments increased substantially, several new buildings went up, and historic campus sites were refurbished. The college's regional image—virtually ghostlike in the early and mid-1980s—was clear, vibrant, and very much alive. Despite its chronically fragile financial state, by 1989 Silver College was a rising star in its community, much to everyone's surprise, with President Book as its acknowledged "miracle worker."

The top administrative team of Silver College represented the full spectrum of team thinking: all the roles were in play, and virtually every team member played more than one role. What was particularly noticeable to an interviewer was that the members of this team described each other in thinking terms. For example, they said that Emily is good at taking apart problems (Analyst), that Sam is good at predicting how the faculty will respond to a certain change (Interpreter), that Francis is good at questioning why the team is doing what it is doing (Critic). While the members of the Silver College team appreciated each other's more standard, functional responsibilities (e.g., in academic affairs, student affairs, business affairs), they spent significantly more time during interviews talking about each other as thinking people who contribute to the collective thought of their leadership team.

Although we did not have the opportunity to observe the Silver College team in action when we visited in 1988–89, we talked at length with each member. While our interviewees spoke to us in words that were clearly their own, the portraits that they drew—of their own and their colleagues' contributions and of their interactive thinking and doing— were very much alike. What follows is a summary of some of what we heard on site.

DESCRIBING DEFINERS

In the eyes of the team, the primary Definer at Silver College is President Book: "[Margaret] has vision. She will create scenarios—for example, the diversity that we are growing into. . . . She wants a student center because she believes that would create cohesion on the campus. And she has a vision about college education in this region of the country." According to her team, President Book is just as good at setting the team's agenda as at "figuring out what *really* needs to be discussed" in order to move it forward.

President Book is very careful, however, to share her defining responsibilities rather than retaining them only for herself. For example, she structures team activities so as to elicit the defining voices of all other team members: When she meets individually with each vice president (a weekly ritual) she asserts that "it is her or his responsibility to bring in a list of what they want to talk about." She adds that for the full cabinet's weekly (occasionally biweekly) meetings, she "tries to ask each one to bring something in" to discuss as well. In this way, she stimulates a teamwide process of defining.

DESCRIBING ANALYSTS

Who fills the Analyst role at Silver College? In short, everyone, including the president, takes a turn at this role, although two individuals—the vice president for business affairs and an associate vice president in academic affairs—are named most frequently.

Individuals in the Analyst role are described as being "very sharp," as having "strong analytical skills," and as "able to see things from many different angles." They are seen as expert in "cutting to the core of a problem" or "going to the heart of an issue." And they are known for exploring and projecting effects. For example, there is the vice president who "always wants to look at the financial impact of an issue." There is the administrator who is adept at "considering impacts on students." And there is the president, who regularly "forces us to look out five to ten years . . . where we will be if we continue to do what we are doing."

DESCRIBING INTERPRETERS

Three individuals, all in vice presidential positions, are in central interpreting roles at Silver College. All three are long-time college members, and two sat on the previous president's cabinet. The third was a midlevel administrator promoted by President Book. Interviewees consistently described these three as bringing a "real historical perspective," a "long sense of history," and a "real sense of what has happened here" to the team's (and particularly the president's) turn-around agenda. In classic interpretive fashion, they are seen as "trying to figure out how the things [we are working on now] fit with precedent . . . and what message we are sending with whatever we are doing [now]."

DESCRIBING CRITICS

The team's Critics include one long-time college member (also in the Interpreter role) and two relative newcomers to the College. Interviewees describe these persons as "strategic thinkers" who "point out that we have to look at some issue that we are overlooking" and who ask "radical questions" like, "What if we don't have a health clinic?" and, "Why [do] we do things as we do?" One of the persons regularly in the Critic role describes himself as "the one who says things that others will not say, telling Margaret things when no one else wants to."

DESCRIBING SYNTHESIZERS

At Silver College, the Synthesizer role is played most often by President Book. For example, some members of the team describe how she engages their participation in setting the team's agenda, and how she establishes a climate of tolerance among them: "We feel free to bring up whatever issues. . . . There is passion, [but] we do not get testy or angry. There is no name calling or stalking off." Others explain that President Book elicits team members' viewpoints and ideas ("she wants honest opinions") critically ("she will argue it with you"). They also describe how, in the end, she draws diverse ideas into meaningful wholes ("she does a wonderful job of framing the issues").

DESCRIBING DISPARITY MONITORS

This administrative team makes extensive use of Disparity Monitors. The president, who is relatively new in office, appears concerned about how others see her leadership, and she asks her team to "keep their ears to the ground" and to "talk to [her] about what [they] are hearing and seeing." She often notes that she wants to "find out people's concerns about the institution" and that "it is very important for her to know that."

Others on the team concur with her concerns, seeking out "information that . . . gets picked up through the informal network, . . . emotional gripes or comments that would never surface in formal reporting lines of the organization, . . . what you hear over coffee."

DESCRIBING TASK MONITORS

Five individuals (including the president) participate in the team's Task Monitoring role. These individuals typically focus on "how the critical path is going," and they are concerned with "getting decisions ordered

in terms of long-range goals." They are often described as group facilitators but with a strong task orientation, for example, having "an endless
willingness to do whatever needs to be done," acting as "the best utility
infielders that anyone could ask for," balancing "process and product,"
and bringing people together for coordinating purposes. The team's Task
Monitors are seen as particularly adept at keeping the group "focused
on issues" while "sorting out what responsibilities belong to whom."
They frequently ask themselves and the team "if what we are trying to
achieve is what we set out to do . . . and are we being economical and
efficient and fair" in doing so?

DESCRIBING EMOTIONAL MONITORS

Three individuals are prominent in the Emotional Monitoring role on
this team: a vice president known for his "great sense of humor"; the
president, who is known for her supportiveness and inclusiveness; and
the president's executive assistant, who "glues" the team together.

The president is particularly strong in mediating relationships. She
describes how "one of the [vice presidents] may come to [her] to say,
'Margaret, I am struggling with my reaction to Sam's style in the group.
Do you have any ideas on how to deal with this?' " And she describes
her desire to "make [people] believe, 'You have a strong relationship with
me.' " She also voices her concern that a new person on the administrative
team be "plugged in" with other team members, and mentions her efforts
"to raise the consciousness about [the new team member] being down
the hall [and separate from the other vice presidents]." The president is
also much concerned about how team members feel about themselves as
a group: "It is getting near time that we should ask that question together:
Is everyone having fun, or just Margaret?"

Silver College is in an unusual position. Its team possesses all eight thinking roles. At the same time, we should note that it did not come by its
team easily. A few top-level administrators came and went during the
earliest years of President Book's tenure. However, from examining the
team process at Silver College and at several other institutions like it, we
are able to conclude that some teams may succeed in building up, within
themselves, a quality of *cognitive complexity*—a collective talent base
that lets team members see and understand college life from multiple
perspectives and to process new information in diverse ways. What can
a president—or for that matter, any team leader—do to convert her or
his colleagues into a cognitively complex team that reflects all or most
of the eight roles? We close this chapter with several suggestions.

Using the Eight Roles to Make
Leadership Teams More Effective

The following are recommendations for improving the collective thinking of a leadership team, thereby heightening its cognitive complexity:

1. Become aware of how your team thinks. Does the team engage in
definition, analysis, interpretation, critique, and synthesis? If so, who
typically sets off each of these processes? Who participates in them, and
in what ways? Are some of these processes more problematic for the
team than others? In what ways? Why? Does the team also have the
three monitoring roles in place (Disparity, Task, and Emotional)? Overall,
which roles and which teamwide processes appear to be missing? Why?
Should the team make special efforts to institute them? How might it do
so?

2. While it is important to note patterns of member participation
within the team, it is even more important to be aware of patterns of
nonparticipation and, in some cases, exclusion. Consider especially
whether one or more persons typically do not participate in certain types
of team process (e.g., definition) or at certain points in team deliberations.
Why may this be happening?

3. In putting a team together, seek out individuals who are particularly
good at some form of thinking (e.g., analysis, interpretation, critique)
and at stimulating it in others but who also can tune into other forms
of thinking and can join in a process initiated by another team member.
The most difficult team members are those who can hear only their own
voice, who can tolerate only their own thinking and points of view, who
have little patience for or interest in the thinking of others, and who can
initiate but cannot follow.

4. Seek out team members who are particularly good at a certain form
of thinking *and* who display a capacity to *learn* other forms of thinking
rather than sticking purely to their own. People on teams can learn to
think in different ways from each other. They can stretch each others'
minds as they try out new thinking behaviors that their teammates model.
In this way they enhance their individual "ways of knowing" as well as
those of the team as a totality.

5. While it is important for the lead administrator or team builder (in
the case of our research, the president) to play the Definer role, it is
equally important that this person encourage other team members to play
it as well. There are some things in the world that presidents and other
leaders (like most people) simply cannot see or understand. Letting others

into the Definer role may permit some of those things to come to light. A team structure that requires members to share the Definer role allows for the possibility that other team members will bring out particularly relevant information. Moreover, a team builder who encourages colleagues to define (and, thereby, to initiate) the team's agenda is likely to heighten their investment in the issues they bring up and to increase their sense of personal power as they engage in creative acts (rather than just processing what "the person in charge" gives to them).

Team builders can encourage team members to play the Definer role in several ways. For example, a college dean might openly encourage a department chair or assistant dean to take the defining lead on a certain issue while the dean plays a more supportive role (e.g., Analyst). This kind of role exchange can send a powerful message to other team members, suggesting, for example, that they, too, might take the defining lead on certain issues. In one of the teams in our study, a president who used this "modeling" approach in conjunction with one of her vice presidents (the VP played Definer while the president played Analyst) showed the other members of the team that it would be "okay to argue with the president" and that it was more than okay to take an initiating stance on the team.

On another study team, the president ensured that individual members would play the Definer role by scheduling regular one-to-one meetings with her vice presidents for which they (not the president) were required to create the agenda. The president then moved what she learned from each vice president to the team's collective agenda for its regular formal meetings. On a third study team, the president designated a large portion of each week's team meeting for the individual concerns or problems of the team members themselves. At these times team members could bring up what they saw as emerging issues. Or they could seek out their colleagues' advice on issues that were brewing within their own divisions, with the understanding that those issues would remain within the purview of the administrator who brought them up, though the team offered insights and advice.

6. Hold regular team meetings because they are the settings in which collective thinking is most likely to happen. People sitting in their individual offices are not likely to think together. Interactive thinking requires interactive time together. Moreover, formal time is as important as informal time together. (At the same time, however, avoid giving out the message that team members are at the beck and call of a "lead administrator" or a person ultimately "in charge." Respect team members' time alone, and also their time in other teams, as much as their time in the team that you are trying to build.)

7. Consider the patterns of thinking on your team, and balance them with care. The team roles represent points and counterpoints. Thus, the views of the Definer, Analyst, and Interpreter may balance (even conflict with) those of the Critic. The Interpreter, who focuses on what she or he knows of the past, may balance or clash with the Disparity Monitor, who focuses on what is happening "out there right now." The Task Monitor, who wants to move the agenda along, balances or strikes against the Synthesizer, who takes time to pull the pieces of the team's thinking together, and also the Analyst and Interpreter, who require time to think through team issues.

The balance may be particularly important in differentiating the needs of new versus experienced administrative and academic leaders. For example, we learned from our study that presidents may be overly attentive to Disparity Monitors (who let them know how they are doing) and to Critics (who give them ideas for new and exciting changes) without giving enough attention to Interpreters, who could advise them on the kinds of things that will and will not work in their particular setting. Veteran presidents, on the other hand, are likely to give a tremendous amount of attention to Interpreters (or to their own well-honed skills in interpretation) rather than attending to Critics or Disparity Monitors. This pattern suggests a need for careful balance: New presidents may have to strain to attend to Interpreters; old presidents have to stretch beyond comfortable interpretation in finding time to listen to the different, perhaps uncomfortable, words of Critics and Disparity Monitors.

While these recommendations may be useful to leaders whose teams are assembled and under way, they may not fully address the needs of leaders who are at earlier stages of the team-building process, or whose fully developed teams are undergoing change. In chapters 6, 7, and 8 we discuss several such considerations in building, maintaining, and reshaping a team, many of which we learned from Silver College as well as from other real teams within the study's sample. However, before we turn to the topic of team building, including the cultivation of a collaborative teamwork ethic, we look more closely in chapter 5 at the factors that differentiate a truly good team from one that is less effective. We consider especially whether having a complex team is a good thing or not.

5

Searching for a Good Team

Of the three team functions—utilitarian, expressive, and cognitive—the cognitive is perhaps the most difficult to grasp because it refers to the team's "mindwork" rather than to its more concrete, observable behavior. Despite its intangible nature, the cognitive function is probably the most important of the three functions. It is also the most complex. Teams that act like social brains—where members actively think together—are likely to display diverse cognitive processes and styles (the eight team roles) configured in equally complex designs.

But while these patterns are intuitively appealing, do they, in fact, matter? Do they make a difference in the quality of leadership? Is the complexity of the multi-function and multi-role team necessarily better, for the people who serve on the team and for the college as a whole, than the simplicity of a team that is oriented purely to utilitarian operations with few thinking roles in place? Several related questions come to mind: Is it really healthy to have so many conflicting viewpoints within a group? Is it not more effective to have just one person (e.g., the president in an executive leadership team, the dean in a college-level administrative team) take the thinking lead while others support, assist, and carry out the directives of this person "in charge"? Shouldn't emotional-support matters be left at home, so that the team can focus purely on its professional tasks? In adding new functions and roles aren't we complicating institutional life so much that we block our abilities to get things done? Why should we muddy the organizational waters more than they are already?

We invite our readers to join us in addressing these questions by looking at the inside experiences of several leadership teams participating in our study and by considering also the state of the institutions in which these teams functioned. In the sections that follow we present summary portraits of team life and campus life for two very different types of top-level administrative leadership groups. We refer, first, to teams that are *functionally and cognitively complex*. These teams are "real" teams in which all three team functions are intact (utilitarian, expressive, and cognitive), and they reflect numerous thinking roles, particularly "core" roles (Definer, Analyst, Interpreter, Critic, Synthesizer). We also consider the opposite configuration—teams that are *functionally and cognitively simple*. These teams, all deemed "illusory," reflect just one team function (the utilitarian) and deemphasize thinking roles. For shorthand purposes, we will refer to these two sets of sample teams as *complex* and *simple*. (A breakdown of our sample, on the basis of complexity and simplicity, is included in Appendix B.) In comparing complex and simple teams we consider the following factors:

- What life is like within these two types of leadership teams; whether they differ in form, style, and quality of teamwork; and whether the differences matter to team members
- What life is like within the institutions in which the teams function; whether one type of team or the other is associated with institutional improvement or development, and the extent to which a team may contribute to this

By comparing the two types of teams from within themselves, and also in relation to the larger organizational contexts in which they are embedded, we hope to arrive at a richer understanding of what it means to have a good team.

Life inside the Team

We begin our comparison of the complex and simple teams in the study sample by listening to the people in them—the teams' members—and we attend especially to their satisfactions and concerns.

The members of the complex teams participating in this study typically rated their teamwork more highly than the members of the simple teams. When we asked them to assess their teams' effectiveness, most members of complex teams hardly hesitated:

It is very, very effective . . . one heck of a team.

I am very happy.

Relationships in the team are very good.

It is strong. . . . I would not trade it for any other.

We are at our peak. It is going real well.

I think that they [other team members] are terrific.

It is affirming and workable.

Although virtually every team had its skeptic, most people on complex teams rated the quality of their teamwork high.

When asked about their team's effectiveness, the members of simple teams often hesitated, referring to what the team "could" or "might" become rather what it is: "I think it could be more effective." Some interviewees were outright negative in their team ratings ("I don't think of us as a team") while others hedged ("It is awfully early to tell. . . . I could answer better in a few months") or simply avoided responding ("I don't know how to answer that").

The members of simple teams agreed less in their self-assessment than the members of complex teams, largely because the president might see the simple team as very positive while other members would not. For example, at one institution the president described his team as "quite good." Other team members were less sure:

VP 1: I think it could be more effective with some direction, with better communication.

VP 2: Fairly good team. . . . [Members] interact well . . . relate well. [But] we don't share a common vision. . . . I don't think we have a defined direction.

VP 3: We have not had the chance to come together and coalesce. . . . We are not a team, but we *are* a team at the same time.

What may account for these different reviews among the members of complex and simple teams? Our interviews indicate that complex and simple teams differ in how satisfied members are with turf designations, time for meetings, and the team's tolerance of and open-mindedness toward cognitive differences.

Turf

The members of complex teams reported little rivalry or contention over who is responsible for what areas or which resources belong to whom. They were clear on lines of responsibility, and although they said that the team argues (perhaps frequently) over who most deserves discretionary monies, they also indicated that they listen to each other's arguments and that they give in gracefully (or try to) when they fail to make their points—or when someone else on the team makes a better point.

What is most characteristic of the complex teams is that there are few, if any, questions about where divisional boundaries lie. These were laid out very early in each team member's term. When we asked a vice president who is a member of a complex team about the extent to which his team is really a team, he responded, "Pretty nearly completely so. No one has an ax to grind. . . . There are no turf issues." This was the typical response from members of complex teams.

The members of simple teams told a different story. Here the boundary lines between academic, business, student affairs, and external affairs divisions were more shaky, and team members let us know that they typically quarreled over and wondered about the scope of their responsibilities in relation to those of others on the team. For example, we heard that at Carson College, one of our sample institutions, the executive vice president sees his responsibilities differently from the way the president defines them, and differently from the way other team members would prefer to think about them. In the words of one vice president: "The executive vice president sees himself as Mr. Inside and all internal operations [including those of the VP who is speaking] are in his portfolio. . . . I don't think that this is how the president sees it but rather that we all have our areas of responsibility and that the executive vice president's is the largest area."

When we interviewed the president of Carson College, he avoided taking one side or the other, stating instead that "to be responsible" he still needs "to shuffle things around" among two vice presidents and the executive vice president. In a later interview, the executive vice president went further, denying that the president's current set of top administrators are the leadership team (even though the president had designated them to us as such) and indicating that soon he and the president would need to establish such a group (although the president never said this to us). In the words of that executive vice president: "The president and I both think that we need a cabinet or some kind of reference group that we don't have now—a team. We will probably do something [about] this." Other members of the Carson College group were aware of this conflict within their cabinet, and they also saw the possibility of other team members "coming to battle" in the near future because each believes that he has authority over "the same [institutional] area."

Time for Meetings

A common characteristic of simple teams was that they rarely met as a whole. There were several reasons for this. Some members of simple teams saw themselves as overwhelmed with individual tasks: "We each have so much on our plates that we work very autonomously and separate." Others explained that they had few meetings because there was no regularly scheduled time for them and, therefore, other matters could take priority. One vice president on a simple team explained, "It depends on the president so that [the meetings] could be at any time"—or as others complained, hardly ever. The members of other simple teams explained that it was easier to keep things straight when they dealt with people one-to-one or in very small groups rather than amid the cacophony of multiple voices. The president of Carson College, and leader of the simple team introduced in the preceding section, explained his "subteam" approach in this way: "John and I work really well together. The same goes for Max and me. And sometimes it is Max and Bill and me. It can also be Martha and John and me. Rather than the five or six of us, it is usually groups of two or three, with me in each of them. When you get the five or six of us together it is not coherent." While the president of Carson College was comfortable with this parceling approach, another member of his team voiced concern: "We ought to meet with some regularity. The president needs to deal with us one on one, but then we don't know what we tell each other. You do have to have this privacy, but not *all* the time. . . . The way to strengthen the group is with more meetings."

The members of the Carson College team, and those of other fragmented teams (all designated as "simple" and as "illusory"), typically rated their teamwork as low—for example, as a "C to a C+," as a "D," or as a "6" (on a scale of 1 to 10)—grades that we never heard from the members of complex teams. It is also important to note that the members of the simple teams frequently described their group as lacking information or communication:

> I think [the team] could be more effective . . . with better communication. The president has never given me explicit feedback.

> [We need] to talk openly about issues, and not to be reacting to issues. [We need] to be ahead of issues. We need to increase communication.

> The uncertainty . . . is the biggest omen hanging over our heads right now.

> We need more data [for] more informed decisions.

In contrast, the members of complex teams were much more comfortable with the quality of communication within the team, both formally and informally:

> We have a lot of interaction. [We] hang together. . . . We call each other if we hear things [and] are in and out of each other's offices.

We talk before we do things.

In a sense, the members of simple teams are "strangers" to each other much more than the members of complex teams. Complex teams meet more often than simple teams, and usually on a regularly scheduled basis. They have a chance to get to know each other and to come to understand each other's hopes and problems. The case of Silver College (see chapter 4) is a prime example: The group meets once a week (actually about three times monthly) as a whole. Each member of the team has one-to-one meetings with the president, and often the issues introduced in the one-to-one meetings reappear on the agenda of the large group. Conversely, issues brought up in the large group may be discussed privately with the president. There is a strong informal bond stretching laterally among the members of the Silver College team, and they often meet together as colleagues and friends, with or without the president, to talk over topics of mutual concern or interest. They are mindful not to alienate members of the team, particularly new people. They are adamant about being open with each other, and about constantly seeking out information to share with one another.

Occasionally, the members of complex teams complained that the number of meetings dropped off during busy times and that this created problems, but even then, the frequency of their meetings was higher than that of the simple teams. Complex teams guarded their times together jealously. When we probed about what made their meetings so important, we heard comments like this:

> If we were concerned about efficiency, we could spend less time together. But there is a lot to be said for building a team by simply being together. We have a lot of bantering among us and joking and kidding—loose and informal. We could cut this out and get to the heart of the agenda, but that would be short-sighted. In this way, we ... build a shared sense of the institution just by talking. The ideas [we talk about] are unstructured and it is where the conversation takes you. We have a shared notion of what we are doing and how to go about it.

Tolerating Cognitive Differences and Staying Open-Minded

As analysts of the complex and simple teams, we believe that a major difference between the two types is the degree to which their members are sensitive to and accept the fact that different people are likely to see the same reality in different ways and to make different sense of it. The members of complex teams are aware—and, in fact, they are proud—

of their internal cognitive diversity. Despite the conflicts that such diversity can breed, most complex teams try to preserve differences, to cultivate them further, and to avoid what some describe as a debilitating cognitive "entrenchment." Two presidents, each working within a complex team, described their views on this:

> I believe in what John Gardener says—you can become mature, entrenched, satisfied, routinized. And that means moving from innovation to maintaining. I don't think that we are there, but there is the danger of us becoming that, and we have to be on the alert that that may be happening . . . that we should become stodgy . . . not challenging one another, not pushing new ideas. It is hard to keep the ideas going.

> It is a good team. We have diversity, which is something we like . . . a good idea group. . . . We don't all get along in the sense [that there are some] personality clashes. But I am sure I would not trade any of them.

We found that in complex teams the president understood and tried to live by the concept that cognitive diversity is a good thing although difficult to manage. While it might be easier for the president to simplify by selecting people who think alike or by bringing people together in more congenial subteams, or simply one to one, the net result would probably be less creative and less useful to the team and to the college as a whole. The result would likely be an illusion of teamwork.

What, then, are the qualities of presidents who put together complex teams? Our research suggests that while these persons are capable of playing several cognitive roles (see chapter 4), they are particularly talented at exercising the Synthesizer role—at eliciting and orchestrating team members' thought processes, melding their views, creating a workable environment, and knowing when it is time to move on. In describing their president, the members of complex teams made comments such as these:

> Before Matthew came, it was not a team. There was no talking. There was no input, just information giving. So he has done a good job. . . . Maybe that is because we had nothing before. We have gotten to know each other.

> Margaret can make things coalesce in a much more informal way than most people can. She is very secure. She is very clear in what she thinks needs to be accomplished and what she can accomplish.

While the Synthesizer role is bound to be important to presidents and others concerned about bringing together the elements of a complex team—for example, in eliciting diverse modes of thinking and in encouraging tolerance for views that differ from the norm—leaders can do other things to extend and strengthen team thinking. Let us consider what this means in the case of the president. As a first step, the president can meet with search committees for top-level administrators to urge consideration, not only of applicants' substantive qualifications (e.g., experience as a professor and scholar, familiarity with academic affairs), but also their experience or promise of working well within a peer leadership group. The president can also structure search processes so as to assure consideration of candidates' abilities to work with others. For example, presidents might request current members of their teams to meet with candidates and to give their impressions to the search committee. Or following the model of one of the teams in our study, the president might arrange to visit the home institution of the top candidate to find out firsthand how others see and feel about the person's style of interaction and collaboration.

Putting together a presidential team can be particularly difficult in colleges and universities where team members are also the official leaders of professional collectivities or staffs, notably the faculty, but also student affairs personnel, the business division, and so on. A professional collectivity such as any of these—but particularly the faculty—is likely to insist upon having a key voice in selecting the chief administrator for its area. While this is completely acceptable and understandable, given the norms and traditions of higher education, the search committee may need to be reminded that the ideal candidate will be just as good at working with peers on the president's leadership team as at leading a professional collectivity.

But what should search committees—and team members involved in evaluating job applicants—look for in a prospective candidate with regard to teamwork skills? Perhaps the most important quality to look for in a potential teammate (regardless of substantive considerations such as the person's expertise in academic affairs, finance, student services, and so forth) is the quality of cognitive tolerance and openness, to which we referred earlier. If the person considered for a job is otherwise qualified to carry out the substantive duties involved, cognitive tolerance and open-mindedness will give him or her a "leg up" in working with other members of the team. At the very least, such a person will be able to participate in the team thinking processes.

We have found in our study that team members who are tolerant of each other's viewpoints are also likely to be respectful of and curious about each other's minds; they might even seek to learn new cognitive skills from each other. We believe that this kind of orientation—cognitive tolerance, acceptance, open-mindedness, and a desire to learn to use one's head in diverse ways—is likely to signal a person worth adding to a leadership team. The expert who knows a content area (e.g., business affairs, student affairs, and so forth) inside out and who is attached exclusively to a particular point of view but cannot enter or explore others' thinking is likely to disrupt the complex team.

The Silver College team described in chapter 4 encountered just such a problem when the college hired a vice president whose mode of thinking differed from that of other team members. An interviewee commented on the experience:

> The former vice president was a strange dude. He saw there to be only one truth and it was his. . . . He wanted to fight when we did not have to. He had no understanding of other areas and did not have the mind to [understand them]. Our process was over his head. . . . [He] thought we needed more focus on outcomes. He alienated people. . . . He needed more formality on the administrative staff and wanted it to be more of an august body. Margaret [the president] had brought him in. . . . We hired him quickly and that was a mistake.

One of the requirements for a complex team is to learn how to tell ahead of time what kind of person will meld well with a group committed to team thinking, and what kind of person will not. We believe that this learning happens most often, as it did at Silver College, through trial and error.

But what are the determinants of a good fit between an existent team and a new person seeking entry to the team? We speculate that what counts is *not* a person's specific substantive expertise (e.g., student affairs, financial affairs) or thinking skills (definition, analysis, and so forth), but her or his openness to learning through team thinking—that is, the person's interest in and commitment to team thinking as a way of team life. We believe that it is difficult to predict the exact thinking role that a new person on a team will play, largely because this may differ from situation to situation in relation to the unique chemistry between a particular person and a particular team. In other words, we suspect that a person will play somewhat different roles on different teams, and that it is often difficult to predict which aspects of a person's "role repertoire" a particular team setting will elicit. What may be known, however, is whether or not a person is open to team thinking as we have described it here, regardless of the specific thinking roles that she or he might come to play on a given team. Persons assessing job candidates for their fit with a complex team that is already in place should make this kind of openness to learning their prime consideration.

How do simple teams compare with complex ones? First, the simple team is more likely to seek cognitive consistency among its members rather than to search purposefully for differences. While consistency would appear to reduce conflict within the leadership group, it actually generates unhappiness and controversy as team members purposely shut out each other's differences, as they become less sensitive to and less accepting of each other's unique ways of seeing and thinking about college matters and focus only on "the company line." We heard several of our interviewees on simple teams talk about how hard it is to deal with colleagues who make "demeaning" statements and about latent and open conflict as team members "come to battle" with each other. We heard calls for more "trust and respect for different points of view" and for more tolerance. We also heard team members describe what it is like to be silenced by a president who, unlike his predecessor, cannot or will not hear diverse points of view:

> We are not a team like we used to be. We are a team in that we work for the same person. We used to be more so. We have a great amount of respect for each other. But now we are implementors. We are the agents of actions [rather than decision makers]. The main agenda point is to get the president's okay. Previously [during previous president's term], we would say, "I want to do this." We were more in control. Now you say, "I recommend." Now you are seeking tacit approval.

It is very likely that in composing simple teams of people who think alike, a team builder is hoping to enhance the possibility of constructing a common team vision. Our study indicates that just the opposite happens. Perhaps because the team builder (i.e., the president) *assumes* a similarity in the team members' thinking, she or he then fails to shape the team's understanding. What results is not more understanding of the team's "reality" but less: "We don't share a common vision. Sometimes I felt that with the former president we had a more defined position. I don't think we have a defined direction [now]. The [new] president may need to provide a stronger position."

In sum, complex and simple teams vary in these ways: The complex team purposefully seeks out cognitive diversity in its members, and it lives by a strong norm of cognitive tolerance and acceptance. The simple team seeks consistency of mind among its members, abhorring the "incoherence" that diverse intellects are likely to bring to the cabinet table. As a result, the simple team is less tolerant of cognitive difference than the complex team.

Let us compare from our study an instance of the president acting as Synthesizer within a complex team with the way the president acts within a simple team. While the president in the complex team plays a strong Synthesizer role, acting like an orchestra conductor who sequences individual musicians for their cumulative effect and assures that each instrument is heard as part of the whole, the president in the simple team disassembles the orchestra to listen and work with just one or two instruments at a time. While the president in the simple team may help the team members perfect their individual performances, she or he is not likely to help them create rich, symphonic sound. The president in the simple team is less a conductor than a regulator. While the resulting technique may be good, the musicians make little real music together.

Other Differences

We found, in our study, that life in complex and simple leadership teams differed in other ways, several of which are related to the issues we have already described. We enumerate these briefly here.

While both complex and simple teams contained "inherited members" (individuals who served on the previous president's cabinet), those who sat on the complex teams were typically better integrated into cabinet activities than those on simple teams. We found that inherited cabinet members on simple teams often felt alienated and confused about "how I will be evaluated" and about the direction the president sought for the team and for the college. They frequently expressed a need for "more communication" and "more information." They were unclear as to where they stood in the eyes of their colleagues, particularly the president.

On complex teams, "inherited members" presented themselves as "chosen" rather than as merely "passed along." We had the impression that even though they had been in the institution all along, their new president had purposefully adopted them as cabinet-level colleagues. They saw themselves, and their teammates treated them, as peers and as valued colleagues.

Lateral support among members was rare in simple teams but frequent in complex ones. Because simple teams were likely to be characterized by one-to-one relationships between the president and other team members, with few lateral or cross-cutting relationships drawing individual members into an organic, weblike whole, each member was at risk of "falling off the edge" when neglected, for whatever reason, by the president. Even a simple spat or unintended reduction in contact between the president and a team member might force a member closer to the outer edge of the team. Moreover, the members of simple teams rarely supported each other laterally as did the members of complex teams.

The leadership team of Taylor College, led by President Geneva

Atwood, illustrates the dynamics of alienation on simple teams characterized mainly by one-to-one relationships. President Atwood's orientation to teamwork was highly hierarchical. She presented herself to us as the source of the team's and the college's ideas, as the institution's intellectual architect, and as its final approving authority: "They [the team] are there to guide and to advise me, to be candid and frank with me, with regard to my leadership, . . . to carry forth to their people my vision and goals. . . . [My relationship with the team] is formal. There is a sense of superior-subordinate, that I am definitely in charge." As these comments suggest, Atwood did not see the team as an organic, interconnected group. Rather, she focused on her own one-to-one relationships with each vice president:

> I tell Belinda that it is her job to package and to sell me. . . . She promotes me and provides entree for me to minority groups and to the media. We work closely together. . . . I think that Julia is real good at telling [me] when things are not going well, and Belinda also. I think Richard will be that way too. . . . I will rely on him for fiscal accuracy. . . . Julia tends to take the opposite viewpoint with me, as do Belinda and Richard.

President Atwood judged the quality of her vice presidents' performance in terms of what they did for her on a one-to-one basis. While Belinda, Julia, and Richard seemed to fit well within her scheme of team leadership, she had trouble with her fourth vice president, David, who came at teamwork differently. David worried, not about President Atwood's needs, but about the problems and needs of the team as a whole. He was very critical of the team:

> The way the structure [of the team] is I don't think that we take an issue and look at it from four or five perspectives. It is usually a question of who talks the loudest and the longest. If people are quiet, you need to draw them in. . . . You need an agenda before meetings to prepare for it. At times the most meaty issues fall under the miscellaneous category. . . . [Our meetings are] really cosmetic. . . . We don't have enough time together. . . . We fail to look at longer-range issues which surface here. We fail to look at early warnings before we have a crisis.

Because Atwood was not responsive to team relationships beyond the standard one-to-one pattern of simple teams, she interpreted David's radically different words and behaviors as reflecting "personal problems," and she inferred that her approach to leadership was "over his head." She concluded, tragically for David and also for this team, that she would "need to find a [new] niche for him [so that] he may resign soon."

What we find particularly sad about David's predicament is that his vice presidential colleagues did not seem able or willing to come to his aid. While they saw him differently than President Atwood did—for example, they described him as "concerned" and as having "strong ideas," as "thoughtful, hardworking," and as making "statements [that] are well thought through"—they did not stand up for him. They did not even try to interpret his unique perspective on teamwork to the president. And they appeared to make little effort to talk with him directly to advise him in his relationship with the president. Having threatened his ties with the president while lacking the weblike safety net of laterally positioned colleagues, David—the team's most cognitively complex member—was on the verge of dropping off his team. What was particularly ironic was that the president viewed David's problem as one of intellectual deficiency rather than rich talent.

While patterns such as this are likely to be destructive to a college and to an individual's career, they are particularly harmful when the person who is shut out is culturally different from other team members—for example, by virtue of life experiences related to the person's gender, racial or ethnic background, sexual orientation, or place of origin. A person who is "on the outs," as David was, loses the chance to develop ideas and viewpoints in a setting of shared minds and thus to grow professionally. The team, in turn, loses the person's unique talents and understandings. In short, the team relinquishes an opportunity to learn from one of its own, in the best sense of *learning*—gaining the ability to see and understand more than what team members already know how to see and understand.

The one-to-one relational structuring of simple teams is also destructive in that it pins the idea of a team and teamwork to the idea of an ever-present, all-knowing team leader—in this example, the president. A team member who has no lateral, peer relationships within the team may become overly attentive to her relationship with the person who is presumably in charge. And this may come at the cost of attention to ultimately more important institutional issues that the team leader knows little about. What is particularly dangerous about simple teams is that the conglomerate of one-to-one relationships can make team members overly dependent on the president's or team leader's sense of whatever is happening, rather than on their own sense or that of their colleagues. In short, when team members restrict their relationships to just one other person, they narrow the scope of knowing and thinking of the team as a whole.

The linear, one-to-one structuring of the simple team in effect erases the possibility that the diverse cognitive roles described in chapter 4 will come into play. The cognitive roles are interactive. They require each other. They play off each other. The confining structure of the simple team is inconsistent with their essential interactive qualities. Moreover, the hierarchical nature of the one-to-one relationships between the team leader and each team member virtually guarantees that the team leader always serves in the Definer role and that other team members rarely have the opportunity to bring their own original conceptions of reality to bear on the team's work. As we have seen, the very opposite happens on complex teams, where the rigid one-to-one structures characteristic of simple teams are replaced by organic and flexible opportunities for talking and thinking together with anyone at virtually any time.

The members of simple teams typically described themselves as so caught up in the affairs of their individual units (academic affairs, business affairs, and so forth) that they neglected to consider the institutional whole; in contrast, the complex teams attended to both the units and the college. The focus in complex groups was clearly on the larger, common good, the institutional whole, their work as a team of colleagues, but in virtually every case the cabinet also made time for individual members to bring up issues from their own units. When the vice president for academic affairs at Constance College brings up a personnel problem that is brewing in the political science department, the team listens and asks questions in an effort to understand the situation. Team members present their analyses and interpretations of what may be happening, and they make suggestions as to how it might be dealt with. But the president never steps in and assumes responsibility for the issue, nor does anyone else. The problem remains the property of the academic vice president, who, however, may aggressively seek out the views of his colleagues. It is likely that before his problem is resolved he will call on his team colleagues again and again for their viewpoints, either in the formal setting of a cabinet meeting or privately and informally.

Simple teams complained about playing "defense" rather than considering meaningful issues in a more "offense"-oriented or playful style. They saw themselves as not getting as much done as they would like, as being caught up in "trivia." Moreover, they were often nervous about what they saw as their team's relaxed posture, and several vowed "to do something about it." The simple team typically aspired to the managerial ideal: be rational; think and plan before you talk and act.

Contrary to what we might expect, complex teams were just as inundated with minutiae as simple teams. The major difference was that the members of complex teams were more relaxed about the fact that they could not always plan "proactively" or be on the "offensive" with problems that came their way, or that they could not always deal with big issues instead of "trivia." Complex teams usually acceded to the nitty-gritty landing in their midst, for example, patiently figuring out, as at Silver College, "who is going to clap erasers," and they realized that time spent just talking or "bantering" among themselves is just as important (if not more so) than their grander planning sessions. The complex teams in this study reflected a counterintuitive perspective on planning—an awareness that institutional leaders do not always plan, strategically or otherwise, before they do, but that rather, through doing they may derive their plans (Neumann, in press a). Moreover, through doing they may derive their sense of what they *want* to do and what is particularly meaningful for them to do. Complex teams accepted the fact that action often precedes or simultaneously accompanies thought (Birnbaum 1988, Schon 1983, Weick 1979).

Our observations lead us to this conclusion: complex teams are less caught up in the quest for rationality than are simple teams. This does not mean that complex teams are more passive; in fact, because of the high level of shared talk among members—however undirected that talk might seem—they are more active and more learning oriented than simple teams. The meaningful difference between complex and simple teams is not one of grand strategy as opposed to trivial pursuit, or offensive tactics as opposed to defensive response. Rather it is one of unconstrained, active, learning-centered engagement, as opposed to passivity born of restriction. Complex teams have discovered that rational management can get in their way and can even induce inaction. What holds the complex team together is its members' common beliefs in what they are all about, derived through constant active thinking and talking within their circle rather than through passive adherence to a grand, externally derived management ethic.

While the complex team brings with it a fair amount of confusion, complication, even chaos, it also brings the potential for creativity—both in thinking and doing. The simple team looks good in the abstract. After all, one would think that having expert, focused "doers" would heighten efficiency and accomplishment while minimizing distraction and conflict. However, while the simple team's strength lies in its focus, this focus may also be its undoing, particularly if it becomes constraining. The idea of constraint is at fundamental odds with the aim of "real" teamwork, which is to exceed the natural limitations of the human mind. Thus, while the simple team sounds like a good idea, it is at best an illusion.

Life Outside the Team: Looking at the State of the Institution

While it is important to consider how a team's complexity or simplicity affects individual team members, their relationships, and the character of the team itself, it is ultimately more important, especially for top-level leadership teams, to consider whether and how the team affects the well-being of the college as a whole. In our study we asked: Is a campus likely to be better off if it possesses a complex or a simple presidential team? That is, is a complex team more likely to do good things for a college than a simple team?

These are very difficult questions to answer because we were able to study the fifteen teams only over a time span of three years, and it is likely to take much longer than that to assess effects, whether direct or indirect. As we have learned from many previous studies (see Birnbaum 1988, Weick 1979), the effects of leadership action are not always immediately obvious. What a team or a person does early on, either in taking a specific action or assuming a particular style of leadership, might have a positive influence on the college at that particular time, but as that initial event cycles through the college over many years it might indirectly induce other effects, some of which may not be so positive.

Century College, one of our study institutions, provides an example of how a president's initial actions reaped immediate positive results that turned sour later in his term. When David Norwood assumed the presidency of Century College well over ten years ago, the institution was hardly known and its financial condition was a disaster. Norwood made it his top priority to build a following of friends and supporters while maintaining a consistently balanced budget. His work in the community and his internal reorganization, aimed at assuring internal efficiency, consistency, and accountability, paid off quickly and spectacularly. In a few short years, the college was financially sound and stable, and while it was not extravagantly wealthy, it reflected good health and academic viability to its regional community. In Norwood's words, "I can't imagine how I got so much done so fast." The key to the unbelievable turnaround of Century College was the president's approach to leadership and organization, which he "discovered" very early in his term: "I gave up . . . trying to do everything. I can't be a detail man—if I tried I would kill myself. . . . After setting goals you have to structure organization to do it well and oversee it. I thought I had to work with the [faculty] senate, academic policy, etc.; then I realized others had to do that." One of Norwood's first steps in office was to institutionalize this philosophy through a highly conservative and technocratic budgetary accounting system held in place by a tough, managerially minded provost. With the budgetary and managerial reins well in place, President Norwood could engage in external development activities.

What happened internally over the years? The results were not obvious immediately, and even when we visited in 1988–89 (more than ten years later), they were muffled. But slowly, through interviews that sometimes ran overtime, people searched for words to describe a mounting dissatisfaction, a growing awareness of alienation, a sense of being stifled. In the midst of a bland explanation of the college's financial security, an academic administrator suddenly broke into a description of how she had been "plodding for years," trying to make the college's financial system fit her department's academic needs. While describing Norwood as "a good fundraiser" with "a lot of energy" who "has done a lot for the college," and the college's provost as "strong, conservative, capable," a faculty leader pointed out to us that the college is awakening to a need for "better contact" with central administrators. A professor complained more openly that because "there is less a sense of community . . . no one knows who is in [the administration building] or what they are doing," that the faculty have come not to care: "They may complain, [but] the next day they will be happy as a clam to be left alone."

As the case of Century College shows, what presidents get in their first few years in office is not always what comes out at the end, assuming that they stay around long enough to see and feel the results of their handiwork. President Norwood's externally oriented and internally distanced style worked wonders in the short run, but in the long run it was harmful to the college's internal life and particularly to the vitality of its faculty.

As we completed our study, we wondered whether the changing effects of presidential leadership, such as those we heard about at Century College, might not be repeated with regard to team leadership: Might complex teams turn sour on an institution after a while? Might simple teams take a turn for the better in the long run? Unfortunately, we could not determine empirically exactly what the effects of the study's teams would be five, ten, or fifteen years down the line. That is, we could not look into the future to see (almost in a clinical sense) whether complex teams would, in fact, lead to improved financial conditions, heightened morale, strengthened governance, or a host of other desirable outcomes. (Although we had several senior presidents in our sample, we could not assess the complexity of their earliest teams because the relevant data were not available to us.)

However, there was something very important that we could see and that we described earlier in this chapter: that the members of complex teams genuinely liked their teams and their teamwork better than the members of simple teams. They did a better job of working together than the members of simple teams. In complex teams "turf" was not a divisive issue. The members of complex teams met regularly and often and therefore understood each other well. They purposefully sought out different ways to conceive of their problems and opportunities rather than imposing rigid definitions on each other. The members of complex teams saw each other (even their inherited colleagues) as equals and as valued thinkers. Their eyes were focused on the institution as a totality. They had come to terms with the fact that while they could not always escape the seemingly trivial nitty-gritty of administration, they could avoid sinking into passivity through active, engaged thinking. We believe that this pattern alone offers enough of a promise to be worth the heartache, energy, risk, and courage required to build a complex team.

But our analyses of the fifteen teams participating in this study suggest that there is even more to tell about the potential advantages, to institutions, of having a president (and others) who strive for complex teamwork. For the most part, we found that the presidents who tried to build complexity into their teams were simultaneously trying to build a similar quality into their larger institutions. In short, what we saw presidents doing with their leadership teams (mini-organizations of sorts) was usually what we saw them doing with the larger organizations within which the teams were encased. What was at issue was not what the team could do for the college but what the president's leadership orientation contributed simultaneously to two organizations—the team and the college. Let's consider the case of Constance College and Carson College from our study.

Constance College

The administrative leaders of Constance College compose a prototypical complex team exemplifying the utilitarian, expressive, and cognitive functions and virtually all the cognitive roles (the Disparity Monitor was weak, however, in this team). The president of Constance, a veteran in his position for well over twenty years, describes himself as having "an ongoing conversation" with the members of his team, and they, in turn, describe the openness and continuity of talk among themselves. In describing their work they refer less to their formal divisional roles than to their qualities of mind:

Alex has a good understanding of the whole [and] will bring the faculty
perspective. . . . Vince sees things from a student standpoint. . . . Mark will
bring a great sense of reality and urgency to problems. . . . I usually put
forward a more optimistic view on what he sees. . . . William is new [and]
has never been in a higher education setting. He comes at things differently. . . . As for myself, . . . I have to be a catalyst, [to] bring divergent
views together. I have to ask the right questions.

The team at Constance College intertwines the utilitarian function with
the cognitive function; that is, it alternates action with shared contemplation until decisions are made or problems solved jointly. But the
expressive function is also prominent. This is a team whose members
argue vehemently among themselves, but they are adamant about not
hurting each other and about keeping each other safe. One vice president
commented on his experience:

I don't have to posture myself to show that I know what I am doing. If I
see that I am wrong on something, I don't feel that I need to dig my heels
in to show that I am right. I can be wrong. . . . That takes trust. . . . I think
that the president's leadership style is such that it lets us be open with each
other in the cabinet. But this is what this means when we sit and talk about
issues: that we have long and protracted, emotional discussions. He has
allowed us to go through that kind of process. And when we walk out of
those sessions, I know that I may have lost my point, but I do walk out of
the door supporting the decision that has been made. The president expects
that.

The ethos of the team at Constance College is shared thinking and doing
bolstered by emotional support, and as these comments show, team members believe that this is, in fact, what their president wants.

The ethos of the college itself is very similar to that of the team, and
people all over campus see the president's hand in it. A faculty member
told us that the faculty want and expect to know about major difficulties
facing their college, that they expect the president to keep them informed,
and that they respond actively and with commitment to such information:

We are a community that thrives and anguishes together. We have a sense
of emotional pain that faculty feel when things don't go well. We feel it if
the college hurts, and not just down in our pocketbooks. We . . . have had
both good and bad news. We have had decreases and increases in the numbers
of students, and we have met and we have failed to meet our fundraising
goals. The faculty follow this. We talk about it as a community. You don't
have a president here who just gives out bad news. He also gives out what
we need to do to deal with it. The faculty then talk about what they need
to do and what may inhibit the college.

Constance College is composed of anything but passive, unengaged, or uncommitted people. Its faculty, like its administrators and its students, watch and listen for news, or they create it themselves, and they respond fully and actively to whatever is happening by thinking and by doing. Moreover, they believe that their leadership encourages this kind of engagement.

In sum, what is true of the team at Constance College—and of the president's role with regard to the team—is true also of the college, including the president's exercise of institutional leadership.

Carson College

Carson College is the antithesis of Constance College, and it is the prototype of the simple team. As we noted earlier in this chapter, the Carson College team is caught up in blustery battles over turf. Team members differ in their understandings of who is responsible for what, and there is even a question in the mind of Carson's new executive vice president as to whether a team exists at all or whether he and the president are about to construct a brand new cabinet. The Carson College team is fragmented. It consists of one-to-one relationships, usually between the president and each vice president, with only a few lateral relationships among the vice presidents, and with no sense at all of a more organic, encompassing whole. What stands out most about this team is its chunked texture. Each team member has her or his section of the pie to care for and protect, the president tries to make the different pieces work together, but no one glimpses the whole.

In describing how the team is most useful to him, the president emphasizes the management of institutional pieces:

> One of their [team members'] responsibilities is accepting responsibility for how things go in their areas. I have to have the feel that Development is going okay ... and so on. I have to have confidence that these people can drive their areas and that they don't need me to check on them. ... The team is most useful in dealing with how the actions in one area may influence the others in the short run and to mediate that.

In describing how the team is least useful, he explains: "It is least useful [when team members are] involved ... collectively ... in long-range issues—like where the institution will be in five or ten years. ... The executive vice president and president are the only two who can work on this in their one-to-one relationship."

One of the characteristics of a simple team is the absence of the cognitive function. Often what we would hear on such a team, usually from an inherited member who had experienced complex teamwork on the previous president's team, was a longing for opportunities (usually meetings) that would let people think together. An inherited member of the Carson team says: "We do not have regular meetings of the whole team, nor are they carefully planned when we do. . . . I wish that we had regular meetings because that way the president can set the tone, and that way we can deal with developing tensions. Otherwise they grow and can explode. . . . I need to be in contact with the others."

In our discussions with faculty we learned rather quickly that the cognition that was missing on the president's administrative team was also wanting in the larger organization. Professors at Carson College have widely divergent interpretations of their realities, or their interpretations are muddled and make them very uncomfortable. For example, some faculty members complain that they have no sense of the state of the college's financial health; "information is not good. . . . We don't get meaningfully disaggregated budgets [but] ratios without explanation."

But their sense of confusion goes beyond finances. In the wake of a recent administrative reorganization, faculty members complain that they "can't get a structural [organizational] chart from the administration." They feel "it's a joke" that they cannot even get a picture of what their reorganized college now looks like. Searching for explanations, they infer that "the problem . . . is not the deans or the department chairs, but the higher levels," and they express "serious reservations about the quality of administration." Others bluntly accuse administrators of shutting out the faculty—both their voices and their thoughts:

> We must have participation in decision making. The pattern here has been top-down order giving. We are shifting to a consultative style. . . . But the question is: What is consultation? The ways in which consultation can be implemented can vary. Participation is not the same as consultation. We want a participatory role in all matters that affect the faculty. Theoretically we have that right.

The faculty of Carson College are frustrated by the mystery and disorder around them, and they wonder if the absence of meaning is a sign of yet other meaning—that maybe "things are being hidden from them," or perhaps it's just that administrators "don't know what they are doing."

As these scenarios suggest, there is an urgency among the faculty of Carson College to participate in decision making, but participation is blocked by the absence of understanding or by blatant misunderstanding. A maze of institutional events seem to come and go with little sense or order about them. At Carson College, the absence of a sense-making function—whether in the form of the president, the team, or another body—is more devastating than the absence of data as such. As other studies have shown us, the need for sense in a social milieu is primary, and its absence can lead to worry and agitation, as in the case of Carson College. Or, as we have seen in other institutions participating in our study, it can lead to apathy and resignation (see Neumann, in press b).

While the morale of administrators and faculty at Constance College is dramatically different from that at Carson College, one pattern is clear: In both cases presidential leadership expresses itself in similar ways within two organizational constructs—within the team-as-organization and the college-as-organization. As we noted in chapter 3, the president's or team builder's orientation is likely to go a long way in shaping the character, tenor, and life of the team. We will say more about these patterns as we reflect, in the next section, on the meaning of a good team.

Reflections on Good Teams

What can we learn from the cases of Constance College and Carson College? When we view these leadership teams within their larger institutional contexts we realize that, as teams, they are probably causing certain things (good or bad) to happen in their larger milieus; some of their results show up immediately, while some metamorphose over many years. But what is even more important in these two cases is that what's happening on the team is happening also in the institution at large—that the team is, in effect, more a *sign* of qualitative institutional change than its active *cause*. At Constance College the change in the team and in the college is toward increased complexity—toward more perception, more thought, more contemplation, more shared belief and understanding. At Carson College, the change, both within the team and the college at large, is toward simplicity—toward a dissipation of sense, a decline in sense making, a dissolving of means and opportunities to come together for purposes of knowing and learning.

But what does all of this tell us about the nature of good teams in particular? Given our inside view of what life is like on complex teams as opposed to simple teams, we conclude that the good team is likely to display an array of functions—utilitarian, expressive, and cognitive— and a broad spectrum of thinking roles with a president and other team participants who are adept at playing the Synthesizer's role. But what is even more important is the finding that while complex teams seem positioned to do good things for colleges over the long haul, even if we can't see their effects right away, they are also likely to serve as signs that the larger organization is taking a turn toward complex thinking and doing. Whatever leadership is being exerted to make the team a team is likely being exerted to make the college a college in the best sense of what that means: the members of complex teams think, open each other's eyes to new sights, and forge new understandings. In short, they learn. It is likely that in becoming more complex, the organization, like its leadership team, is also beginning to learn.

In the following chapters, we address what leaders can do to foster teams that learn by virtue of their complexity.

6

The Relational
and Interpretive Work
of Team Building

It is important for leaders to be able to differentiate between real and illusory teams—that is, between complex and simple teams—but it is also important for them to know how to build a team in the first place, how to cultivate its talents, and how to maintain it. In this chapter we focus on the role and responsibilities of the team builder—the person who decides that a team is wanted or needed and who possesses the resources to put a team together. While we refer, in this chapter, primarily to the president as team builder, we believe that much of what we say is applicable to others (e.g., vice presidents, deans, department chairs, faculty leaders) who, like presidents, try to build leadership teams.

As we pointed out in chapter 5, presidents or other team leaders often build teams that reflect their approach to leadership generally, including whether or not they believe in teamwork at all. By virtue of the bureaucratic structure that defines, at least partially, the nature of most higher education institutions today, presidents, more than other institutional officers, are in a position to decide whether they should have a team in the first place. Needless to say, presidents are also in a position to garner resources to shape the type of team that is consistent with their beliefs about leadership and management, even though, as others enter the team, their conception may not be the only one at play (Neumann 1991c). However, in the very act of initiating the team, presidents have the potential to contribute in a major way to the team's character and culture. That is, how they carry out their team-initiating and team-building responsibilities—for example, by assuming a collaborative, interactive style or a unilateral, authoritarian approach—is important because their style of team development is likely to become incorporated, at least to some extent, within the team's culture.

Our study suggests that presidents rarely come to the job with previous experience and training in team building. They typically select their top administrators with a great deal of care and deliberation because they believe that their effectiveness depends as much on the skills and abilities of their administrative colleagues as on their own. However, once this administrative selection process is complete, things can change. Many presidents operate on the assumption that as long as their top administrators are skillful and responsible within their own domains of responsibility (e.g., academic affairs, student affairs), they will coalesce naturally into a team. Quite to the contrary, our study reveals that "real" teams—those that are functionally and cognitively complex—are the product of deliberate team-building efforts orchestrated by the president. They are not just the result of mystical or naturally occurring "bonding" processes.

Certain circumstances encourage the natural coming together of a team. For example, an out-of-the-ordinary event, such as a great crisis or tragedy, is likely to demand joint and cooperative action among team members. One of the colleges in this study provides a sad but helpful example: The meaning of teamwork became particularly vivid to the top administrators of Dryland College when a sudden fire claimed the life of a student athlete trapped in a burning dormitory. Faced with their own despair, and that of the campus, these administrators "had to come together to deal with the unexpected tragedy and to help students and faculty through the process of grieving . . . to put the pieces back together."

Crisis has a way of intensifying the feeling that people need to work together, and on a team, crisis can bring even the most vehement of turf battles to a halt, if only temporarily. However, we found that after the crises had passed, the presidents of "illusory" teams (those with a simple utilitarian function) typically returned to concerns of how best to contain the specific administrative tasks of individual team members. As a result, these presidents were not able to sustain the spirit and momentum of collective action that had marked the crisis, and they lost a chance to transform their groups into real teams. One interviewee described, with regret in his voice, how a recent campus crisis forced administrators to work as a team, but how once the crisis passed, so did the urge to collaborate: "We passed through the Valley of the Shadow of Death. You never saw a group of people more determined to make things succeed. Since then the team has become fractured; the president does not call senior staff meetings anymore." While a naturally occurring circumstance may lay a foundation for teamwork, it still takes deliberate effort to build the team.

Team building is often associated with traditional managerial skills such as selecting and assessing personnel and organizing staff resources and activities, including efficiently conducting meetings, developing productive agendas, and cultivating group decision-making skills. In this book, we purposefully depart from this managerial tradition. We have found, in our studies, that most new presidents have a fairly comprehensive working knowledge of rational management and that what most of them need (and what those who survive gain) is an understanding of the human and sense-making aspects of their jobs (Neumann 1989). Through experience, and from mistakes, presidents learn that they need to attend to their personal relationships to faculty, trustees, and importantly, their own administrative teams (Neumann 1990a). In this chapter we consider what presidents can do, in terms of their own thinking and doing, to build connectedness into their teams and to foster mutual understanding among the people who compose them.

The Team Builder's Mind-set: Individualistic or Team Oriented?

What makes developing a group of individuals into a team a formidable challenge? Why do many groups fall apart? Why do we understand little about the meaning of team-oriented leadership?

The answers to these questions hinge on a point made in chapter 2: traditionally, our field has tended to conceive of leadership in purely individualistic terms rather than as the interactions of individuals, or more globally, the workings of collectivities. The prevailing professional discourse, most of which is based on conventional conceptions of leadership as an individual act, depicts the leader as standing apart from (often above) the rest of the organization and assuming a global perspective that others, by virtue of their lesser abilities, knowledge, or position, do not or cannot share. Conventional leadership theory views the leader as all powerful and as possessing visionary capabilities and goal-setting skills that may seal the fate of an institution. Moreover, it views the strong and distant leader as ensuring the survival of the organization (Bensimon 1991a) by drawing on unique talents and capabilities, by exercising power, or by enacting specialized behaviors (Bensimon, Neumann & Birnbaum 1989).

We believe that presidents and other team leaders whose minds are attuned to a heroic image of leadership are not likely to understand or to try to create teams as we have presented them here—that is, as complex, brainlike entities that are more than a simple mechanistic sum of their parts. We believe, further, that presidents who work from two such divergent notions of leadership (individualistic versus collective) are likely to build dramatically different teams.

We assert in this chapter that it takes altogether different skills to build the team-as-culture as opposed to the team-as-athletic-group, a point we introduced in chapter 2. From a cultural perspective, the team builder strives to access a group's themes, including its mood, the nature of intragroup relations, and the norms that guide decision making. This is very different from a model, such as that of the machine or the athletic team, that typically strives to make the parts of the team work together effectively, efficiently, and smoothly. We propose that team building depends not on the team builder's skill in instrumental management but on his or her relational and interpretive abilities. We *do not* believe that good team building focuses on the coordination of prescribed roles, as intimated by the athletic-team metaphor, but rather on the enactment of processes for engendering connected, collaborative, interactive, and inclusive group work. We describe here several leadership approaches for facilitating such teamwork. We also describe several blocks to teamwork.

The Relational Work of Team Building

From a cultural perspective, team building involves building relationships. This includes creating a team structure that fosters connectedness, interaction, and collaboration. It also requires relational work. We use the term "relational" purposefully to underline that team building demands turning attention away from the self and toward others.

Viewed culturally, the primary aim of team building is not to create a smoothly functioning group (e.g., one whose dominant functions fall in the utilitarian domain) but rather to give meaning to the concept of *team*, including what a particular team stands for and how it enacts this. We define the work of team building as relational to make the point that teams and teamwork are achievements of human beings who work together, rather than outcomes of impersonal managerial processes.

Building a Connected Team: Encouraging Openness, Vulnerability, and Self-Disclosure

A vice president in one of the study's highly connected teams described his group as follows: "We have a lot of interaction. We are protective of each other. We hang together. We have a team identity. We call each other if we hear things. We are in and out of each other's offices a lot. We do things together socially. We have retreats together. We have gone sailing together." The vice president's words capture a connectedness that many administrative groups find difficult to achieve. The tendency of most administrators is to join a group and to assert, simultaneously, their independence from it. Indeed, it is highly unlikely that many members of administrative groups would see themselves as "beings-in-relationship" (Maher 1985).

What does it take to foster a feeling of connectedness among the members of a group? In part, the answer to this question is provided by Karl Weick's observation that "interpersonal authenticity and self-disclosure often solidify ties while simultaneously uncovering the reality of interpersonal difference. People feel closer to those about whom they know more and who they see as fallible, vulnerable, trustworthy, and reliable" (1983, p. 49).Shirley Chater, president of Texas Woman's University, explains how this can be accomplished in a higher education context. Soon after assuming office, she told her cabinet that their meetings should be seen as times when "you can take risks, [when] you can make a mistake and it won't be held against you for the rest of the year." She advised the members of her cabinet, "Be candid, be open, and be vulnerable" (Norman 1988).

Connectedness among team members may be achieved if the president displays a leadership style that encourages (even rewards) self-disclosure among peers. A vice president in one of the study's connected teams put it this way: "I think that the president's leadership style is such that it lets us be open with each other in the cabinet. This means that we have long, protracted, and emotional discussions. He allows us to go through that kind of process. And when we walk out of those sessions, I know that I may have lost my point, but I do walk out of the door supporting the decision that has been made." This vice president (along with his colleagues) sees the president as responsible for setting a tone that welcomes openness. When we visited with the members of fragmented teams we heard just the opposite—that the president inhibited openness.

Needless to say, in an atmosphere where members feel free to express their thoughts openly, we are as likely to hear positive as negative comments. One vice president told us: "We are honest with each other, but honesty is easy if you are dealing with nonthreatening issues. But if [issues] are unpleasant, rather than beat around the bush we try to say so." Openness increases the possibility of acrimony and heated exchange yet, in the long run, is probably less harmful to the team than the pretense of openness. We found that when a team purposely suppressed conflict and unwelcome information, relationships suffered. One interviewee told us, "We have to recognize that as long as we persist in the practice of leaving controversial things off the table we will not be a team." He attributed his team's propensity to evade controversy to a lack of trust and respect for different points of view. We heard just the opposite from a member of one of our more connected (and complex) teams, Silver College: "Our liking each other goes beyond the emotional piece. We have a lot of respect for each other. Therefore, this becomes a team that can have fights." At Silver College, intrateam conflict and argument were expected and accepted.

Declaring that one welcomes openness is one thing, but acting in ways that are clearly consistent with this stance is another. We have found that presidents who consistently foster an atmosphere of openness within the team exhibit two characteristics: (1) they are sensitive to and appreciate interpersonal processes, and (2) they have good understandings of themselves. In building a team it is not enough to state what one prefers in the way of norms, atmosphere, or style. The team builder must also communicate these wishes and intentions through personal action or other nonverbal means. In this way, team members understand that the president truly means what she or he says. This is particularly true with regard to generating a sense of openness within the team. By modeling openness as well as talking about the need for it, the president is likely to assure group members that they can express themselves openly without fear of reprisal, ridicule, or alienation.

When presidents' behavior belies their words, team members become confused and frustrated. One of the presidents in our study reported a style of encouraging openness within the team. In this president's words, "I like people who push against me." But the members of the team saw and heard an altogether different mode of leadership, one that, in the words of a team member, "does not invite challenge, [is] too aggressive, somewhat combative and confrontational." We do not believe that this president was being deceptive with us. Rather, it was clear that the president did, indeed, value and strive for openness. The problem was (as it often is) that what the president espoused was not altogether congruent with how the president acted, or with how others perceived the president's actions (Bensimon 1990b). This particular team presented itself to us as among the most fractured in the sample and clearly as a model of simple, utilitarian functioning. As this example illustrates, the challenge for leaders who strive to build teams is to find ways of determining how others on the team see them.

Connectedness is made possible by feelings of caring. Caring—its presence or absence—is conveyed in a variety of ways. Within a group, caring is communicated by a president's verbal and nonverbal gestures toward the members of the group, or toward the group as a whole. Caring is shown by demonstrating interest in what others have to say without being judgmental or instantaneously evaluative. We learned that one of the presidents in our study responded immediately with negative, non-verbal gestures to comments from team members that were inconsistent with his views or preferences. His tendency to evaluate instantaneously without listening and turning ideas over in his mind deterred openness. "Before you get the chance to present the full argument," a vice president told us, "he wrinkles his nose so you know that he does not want to hear it." In addition to silencing the person who dares to speak up, the president's negative gesture informs other team members that the point is not worthy of their attention. Even if others share the speaker's view-point, it is highly unlikely that, after getting the president's message, they will risk a similar rebuff.

In a noncaring and disconnected climate the potential of the team to think openly, creatively, and complexly is severely curtailed because peo-ple restrain themselves and each other. In the long run, everyone loses out: A facial gesture denoting disapproval brings a potentially useful discussion to an end. The team member who is rebuffed feels alienated and, in the future, will think twice before saying something that might elicit disapproval. When one team member is rebuffed frequently, others learn to discount that person's words ("She is not someone the president listens to"). Under these circumstances the players concentrate more on figuring out the president's "emotional buttons" so as to avoid the embar-rassment that comes with pushing them than on the substance of issues discussed. They are, in effect, distracted from the possibility of engaging in real teamwork.

Caring can also be shown in how one listens—in seeing "the expressed idea and attitude from the other person's point of view, . . . sens[ing] how it feels to him, . . . achiev[ing] his frame of reference in regard to the thing he is talking about" (Rogers & Roethlisberger 1952, p. 29). Defined this way, listening requires more than processing information. It means engaging in sympathetic reflection (Smircich 1983) and feeling the emotions—whether anger, frustration, satisfaction, or commitment— embodied in the language and action of others.

Caring can be communicated through a host of other nonverbal ges-tures. From the following comment, we get a glimpse of how a team might see a president who is not particularly sensitive to the nonverbal messages she gives off: "There are times when we are around the table and she will get up to make a call or will shuffle papers on her desk and leave us hanging. The message we get is that she has made the decision or that we not important." This observation could easily lead one to believe that this president thinks little of the team—a conclusion that could undermine the commitment to work together as a team.

The examples provided here describe how the person in the team-building position may, without knowing it, subvert group processes through gestures that devalue individual or group contributions. We do not offer the concept of connectedness as a means to offset team conflicts. Conflict is inevitable, even healthy. It is the stuff that makes change possible, and teams should be concerned with making change happen. Nor is our concern with connectedness based on a wish to make teams more cohesive. In fact, we are suspicious of cohesiveness because too much of it makes a team susceptible to groupthink (Janis 1972), a phenomenon we discussed at length in chapter 4. Rather, we view connectedness as providing the foundation that makes complex and creative thinking (i.e., real teamwork) possible and tolerable. Simply put, in a climate of connectedness and openness one is less likely to practice self-censorship. There is little fear of saying the wrong thing. In a connected team, people feel free to voice their thoughts, and in doing so, they generate more thoughts and build on each other's thinking. In brief, a team's sense of connectedness appears to heighten its expressive function (see chapter 3), which, in turn, appears to support cognition—that is, the dynamics of "team thinking" described in chapter 4.

Building a Collaborative Team: Empowerment and Nonhierarchical Thinking

Collaboration, as we use the term here, means getting a team to develop a sense of shared responsibility for what the group is doing. This is possible only when group members willingly invest themselves in the making and maintenance of a team. While collaboration sounds like something everybody should be doing, we present this warning: collaboration cannot be initiated through fiat. It cannot be legislated or imposed. It cannot be delivered as a "canned" product. The road to collaboration is neither glitzy nor direct.

The following story from a setting outside our study illustrates our point. A high-level executive recently explained to us how his boss, on completing a week-long training seminar on the dos and don'ts of teamwork, immediately called together his work group. Fired up by his own very positive professional development experience, the boss (who is notoriously authoritarian—a true exemplar of top-down leadership) quickly briefed his staff on what he had learned and proceeded to administer to the staff members several of the self-diagnostic procedures he had completed during his week away.

It was clear to our friend that his boss was eager to share his new knowledge of how to work collaboratively. But it was also clear to *us* that our friend was baffled by what all this meant and what he and his colleagues were supposed to get out of the exercise. As we heard this story, several questions came to mind: Can a team achieve collaboration when they feel they have no say about it? Shouldn't there first be a thorough, open, and honest discussion of how the group has been operating *before* engaging in self-diagnosis? Shouldn't there be a discussion of what collaboration means to each member of the team? Shouldn't the team consider what changes a new collaborative style would entail with regard to the team's current mode of interaction? Is a canned self-diagnosis of one's own leadership style truly a good indicator of one's predisposition to collaborate? Wouldn't a more open dialogue with one's peers and subordinates about how each experiences the other be more helpful and insightful? Finally, and this is particularly important given our focus on teams as cultures: Shouldn't the diagnosis of individuals' propensities to collaborate (or their styles of collaboration) be accompanied by an assessment of the group's norms and practices collectively? Shouldn't the group give as much attention to what members invoke jointly and interactively, as opposed to pinning the cause of a group's style on what one particular person does?

Our concern with regard to this last question is that by focusing purely on an analysis of self (whether in the form of self-diagnosis, or the diagnosis of self by others), we forget that a group's way of working together is shaped as much by collective acts as by individual behaviors, and that often the group's collective enactment of its "groupness" may affect what individuals do, including how they construe what is going on around them. In the spirit of a cultural perspective on teamwork, we urge an emphasis on collectivity, rather than looking only to praise or blame individuals for what they do or don't do within the group.

Although our friend's boss should be credited for bringing the topic of team collaboration to the table, instilling an ethos of collaboration calls for a different approach. It requires the capacity to step out of one's official role. It also requires an authentic desire to share power with other members of the team. An ethos of collaborative teamwork demands a lessening of status differences. One way to make this happen, as chapter 4 shows, is to have the president (or any team builder) encourage other team members to share the Definer role or to assume the role of team Critic. In this way, all team members assume active responsibility for shaping (or reshaping) the team's agenda.

We saw little evidence of collaborative relationships in cases where the president retained firm control of the team agenda, thereby reserving the Definer role for herself or himself. Expressing a desire for informality, one of the teams in our study always convened meetings without first issuing a written agenda. It was purported that team members could bring their own items to the table as needed. However, this team rarely discussed anything other than the president's concerns. As one member told us: "We always begin with the president's items, and that often takes the whole meeting or one-third of the meeting. Even though we try to go around the table to our items, we never get through the process." Members of another administrative group told us that because the president maintained control of the agenda, collaboration was a nonissue. The sole purpose of team meetings was to address the president's needs and concerns: "We meet every week with the president. We cover whatever the president wants; it is his agenda. The purpose of the meeting is to keep the president informed and to have input from all of us."

In both of these cases the absence of an agenda prepared in consultation with team colleagues (i.e., sharing the Definer role) meant that control of the agenda remained securely with the president. The end result was the same in both situations: the team meeting became the president's forum exclusively. Other team members felt no sense of ownership of the agenda, the meeting, or the team.

Collaboration calls for a new conception of human relationships in "posthierarchical" designs (Zuboff 1988). In terms of higher education leadership, it requires reconceptualizing what *power* means, including rethinking the nature of interpersonal relationships among administrative officers and the president. Zuboff's conception of posthierarchical relationships views power as fluid and regenerative rather than, conventionally, as scarce and subjugating. Looking at organizational power in this way is far more conducive to collaboration because, as Shirley Chater has pointed out, "It is not as if there is a fixed amount; . . . the more power you give the more you generate" (Norman 1988).

But what exactly does it mean to work collaboratively? For an inside example, we turn to the administrative team at Dryland College where we listen to a vice president describe the team's collaborative work mode:

> We have a special occupational program that runs 365 days per year. But the college shuts down its dormitories and food service during holidays. Some of the students in the program come from [a distant location]. They have no money or homes. So this affects my area because I have to make arrangements in terms of housing and food. The vice president for academic affairs is also affected in terms of programming. And the other vice presidents are affected as well. So, we brought this issue to the team: What do we want to do about it? We looked at the people who will be affected. We looked at the college's policies. When we face issues like this one there is a lot of discussion. Often, we do role playing of student-related concerns and that helps us anticipate situations. We hash and rehash the situation. We consider

the consequences. We look at all sides of the issue. Then we make a decision and stand by it. We have each other's support.

A collaborative work mode enables the Dryland College team to look at a specific issue in its wholeness rather than segmentally. The team's collaborative mind-set makes it possible for individuals to think beyond the boundaries of their individual areas of specialization and functional responsibility (their "turf").

Additionally, what works particularly well among the Dryland College team is their open-ended problem-solving approach: The team's discussions are not purely informational. Nor are they purely task driven or bounded, for example, with vice presidents concerned about limiting what each might do in resolving problems that do not belong exclusively to any one of them. Rather, team members focus on ideas and on what they can do collectively about problems that belong to all. Karl Weick (1979) says that when people use the plural pronoun collective sense making is under way: note the repeated use of "we" by the vice president at Dryland College.

Based on our examination of numerous leadership studies, and on our analysis of the fifteen colleges participating in this project, we believe that an important outcome of collaboration is empowerment. But we also believe that feelings of empowerment drive collaboration. Rather than thinking of power as control and domination, we urge presidents to think of it as corresponding "to the human ability . . . to act in concert" and to realize that power "is never the property of an individual; . . . it belongs to a group and remains in existence only so long as the group keeps together" (Arendt 1972, p. 143; quoted in Greene 1988, p. 134).

If collaboration is such a good idea, why don't more teams use it? The answer is straightforward: a number of barriers stand in the way. First, many presidents remain deeply committed to authoritarian leadership and their own controlling voice and hand, including the president who informed his team, "I consider ideas and [support] the exchange of ideas, but I will make the final decision." Some presidents simply won't support collaborative efforts, going so far as to impugn the integrity of group decision-making processes. A member of one of the study's teams related just such an incident:

> We [the team] talked a lot about how to best distribute the x percent of the budget that the governor just returned to us. We had to decide the principles we'd use to distribute the funds, and so we worked on that a couple of weeks ago. But then, after all that work, we found out that the president had already met with the faculty and told them his ideas on the distribution of the funds.

This president's unilateral action, and particularly his inattention to the team's efforts, sent a message that he was not taking their "doing and thinking" seriously, that he had already single-handedly "made up his mind about the distribution of the funds," and that the team had no voice in the matter. The team, of course, felt disempowered and skeptical: Why bother with collaborating when your work is ignored?

Team builders can also put up barriers to collaboration by virtue of the team climates they perpetuate. For example, one president in our study defined his team as "an interesting combination of competitiveness and combativeness—but in a friendly atmosphere," and he added, "The vice presidents are turf protective, but they work it out among themselves." While this president was pleased with his team's structure (he referred to it as a reflection of "my militaristic style"), the other members of the team learned to live within it by working in isolation—by going to great lengths to avoid issues that would require working with peers whom they did not altogether trust. A vice president described for us what life inside this team was like:

> We are not very willing to recognize the problems of areas other than our own. This happens because people have hidden agendas [and] play politics. If you do something jointly with someone, you don't often get the credit. It's subtle. When you have two people working jointly to produce something together, one person can hog the credit in front of the president, especially if the results are positive.

In sum, when presidents hold tightly to their authority, collaboration suffers, depriving the team and the president of the benefits of creative and complex thinking and real teamwork. Regrettably, some of these presidents do not know that they do not share power as much as they might. Others are aware that they are purposefully withholding power from others. These presidents define "good leadership" as forceful and directive, and in their teams it is lodged exclusively in themselves. Their aim is to remain "in charge." We speculate that many of these presidents are also not aware of the resentment and dysfunction that their style engenders. Perhaps they don't care, or perhaps they put so much effort into maintaining control that they are blind to what goes on around them. Our conclusion is that most are simply not aware of the possibilities that they and their teams have lost. The members of their cabinets often act out their resistance by adopting a compliant but indifferent attitude and by doing no more than what is formally expected of them: they go to meetings, give progress reports, show loyalty, and back up the president, but they do not think together as a cognitively complex team, and they generate few new ideas.

Building an Interactive Team:
Strengthening Interdependence

In an interactive team, members see themselves as capable of contributing to institutional decision making. While individual team members may speak to the needs of their particular units, they are equally concerned with the needs of the whole. The operating norms of such teams emphasize groupness and promote interaction. An administrator described the "unspoken" rules of teamwork at Silver College (the prototypical "complex team" described in chapter 4):

> Talk to the issues. No personal attacks. Be upfront. No behind-the-scenes politicking before it comes up on the table. This is a team and not a representational model; you are not here as a spokesperson for your area to fight for your interests. Show your understanding of the other person's area and position, and empathize with the problems they are having. Be a real good compromiser. Keep your mouth shut once the administrative staff meeting is over.

As this interviewee pointed out, the tendency of team members to act only as spokespersons for their organizational divisions can be a serious impediment to the building of an interactive team. Rather than forming wholes, such teams are often fragmented. The texture of their discussions feels compartmentalized: topics do not blend, and team members stand separately and apart, literally and figuratively, as they address their comments only to the person deemed to be in charge.

Presidents who construe their team's function as primarily utilitarian, and who view the team narrowly as a purveyor of information, are likely to have noninteractive teams. A salient characteristic of the noninteractive teams participating in this study was that their presidents typically attended to lines of one-to-one communication between themselves and individual members of their teams while abdicating responsibility for lateral communication to other members of the team. Without a structure for promoting interaction among all team members, the relationships that arise occur mostly by chance—for example, because people happen to have offices next to each other, or because circumstances bring certain people together who, by chance, realize that they like each other or that they share certain values.

We found that when presidents focused mostly on their one-to-one relationships to individuals without fostering lateral relationships among team members, teamwork became fragmented. When visiting with such teams, we would see, not a whole, but a string of dyads, triads, and lone individuals. This pattern was common among simple teams, in which the illusion of teamwork was stronger than the reality.

What all of this suggests is that unless a president is actively involved in building a complex web of internal relationships, both between the president and others and among others with or without the president, it is unlikely that the administrative group will develop into an interactive, interdependent team. The case of White Lake College, one of our sample institutions, is a compelling example of a group that wanted to become interactive, if only their president would take the lead. The White Lake team comprised two officers inherited from the previous administration and three officers just appointed by the new president. We learned from the newly appointed members that they strongly valued the idea of team-work. They very much wanted to be able to look at issues from an institution-wide perspective and were concerned that all they heard were insular divisional views. One new officer told us: "Our functioning as a group is still not apparent. I am anxious for the sense of interdependence to grow, because I have to feel free among my senior colleagues to talk openly about harebrained ideas, to criticize and be criticized. Otherwise there is no one with whom you can examine the panoply of issues." The other two new members said as well that the team did not measure up to their desire for tighter coupling:

> Ideally, I would like to see it as a place for institution-wide issues [to] be discussed with a certain amount of candor. A team needs to know the major issues. While I do not have responsibility for academic programs, I should be able to contribute. We need to examine, as a group, where our energies are going.

> I don't think senior officers should just manage their areas. They need to look at the institution through multiple lenses, [from the perspectives of] parents, legislators, and students. They need to understand that no one of us has the only possible view. There are times when we have to put down the BS and say, "We have to approach this as a unified team." The issues we bring to the group should be ones which we cannot do something about single-handedly [but that] need a collective opinion.

These three newest members of the White Lake team were eager to solidify their ties, establish interdependence, and develop a spirit of interactive-ness. What kept this from happening?

The new members pointed to the inherited members. "Their agendas," one said, "are heavily guarded . . . [and] they use institutional history and memory as a justification for maintaining the status quo." One new member described a key inherited member as "coming from the Dr. Lane [former president] philosophy," which represented a time when "senior officers protected their turf, the president [played] quarterback, and the team [acted as] defensive linemen."

When we turned to the inherited members, we heard, quite ironically, a call to "bring larger issues to the table"—something that they said happened during the previous president's term but that they saw as coming to a stop under the college's new leadership. According to one inherited member, "The weakness of the cabinet is that we do not have enough of a traffic cop to force discussion of major elements. We tend to be nitty-gritty."

Without the opportunity to observe this team over an extended period of time, it was impossible to determine just how problematic the inherited members really were. However, what is instructive about the White Lake team is that everyone—newcomers and inherited members alike—saw the need to become more interactive. Moreover, all were in agreement that the president would have to intervene. And they had several suggestions as to what the president could do to "get the ball rolling," including: eliciting the opinions and perspectives of individual team members, planning for the institution as a whole rather than for just one division at a time, focusing on team members as people rather than as functionaries, instilling shared teamwide concern for what appeared to be just one person's responsibility.

Let's turn briefly to Dryland College, where we find a very different team—one that is highly interactive, collaborative, and complex in its thinking and doing—and that displays a very different team-building approach. In the words of a vice president:

> Last Wednesday we talked about the budget not being where it needs to be. I knew it would be discussed. It was an agenda item. The budget probably is not where it should be, in terms of the reserves we would like to have at the end of the year. So the president brought up the topic. We went around the table, and he asked each of us for our views and solutions. Each of us contributed to the discussion.

As brief as this description is, it contrasts sharply with the noninteractive and noncollaborative teams we presented earlier. First, the members of the Dryland College team are well informed as to what is going on in the institution; they are not simply stuck in their individual areas. In this case, they focus on the state of the college budget, which they cast as a team problem rather than the president's individual problem or the finance officer's problem. Second, team members get advance notice of the meeting agenda, a practice that allows them to prepare for active participation in discussion; they are not simply the pawns of the president's agenda. Third, the president encourages and facilitates interaction by inviting team members to contribute their views on institutionwide problems. In building turn taking into the ritual of teamwork, and in promoting cross-team talk, the president of Dryland College is building up a storehouse of team customs: Team members become accustomed to airing their views in team meetings, and just as importantly they become accustomed to hearing each other's perspectives on problems. They grow accustomed to expressing their minds to others and to receiving the views of other minds. By establishing a context of interaction, the president builds a spirit of interdependence into this group.

It is common knowledge that many presidents and others in team-building positions do not engage with their teams in this way. One example of noninteraction, while fictional, nonetheless reflects a common group dynamic. Toward the end of a long and highly structured team meeting covering numerous topics, the convener's seemingly sincere request for the group's input on a routine administrative decision is met with what he deems an inexplicable silence. No one responds to his request. The convener feels frustrated, and understandably so, by the group's blatant indifference, especially because group members had been complaining to him that they were not being consulted enough. Afterward, in speaking to members of the group, the team's external observer, a visitor to the campus, learns that the convener has, in fact, been consulting regularly with group members. However, the issues that the convener typically chooses for consultation matter very little to the group. According to group members, the convener purposefully excludes his colleagues from truly important decisions—for example, those signifying substantial commitments of time, personnel, and resources. "To show you what we mean," one group member says, "immediately before asking us for advice on that silly matter, he informed us of a new programmatic thrust that we never discussed. It was news to us. He just announced it. He said it's a done deal."

From this group's vantage point, the convener's attempt at consultation stands as pretense. While the convener welcomes the group's opinions on mundane issues, he silences them on important decisions. He does not bring important decisions forward, nor does he open the door to the shared defining that would let issues that matter to the team surface. When the group falls silent in response to the leader's request for input, once more on a mundane matter, they are not showing disinterest or indifference. Rather, they are communicating disapproval. They are protesting the way this leader and his organization work. Moreover, because the agenda is full, the members of this team have no opportunity to introduce their own preferred agenda items.

In many colleges and universities around the country, administrators set up special commissions, committees, study groups, and task forces to address a variety of institutional problems or concerns and to tender recommendations for action. While this often represents participatory governance at work, the extent and quality of participation may be judged in terms of several questions drawn from the model of team thinking presented in chapter 4: (*a*) Given the parameters of its charge, to what extent do group members participate in defining the group's agenda? That is, to what extent does the group share the role of Definer? (*b*) To what extent are group members free to question or revise an established agenda? That is, do members assume the role of Critic, and does the group engage in a process of critique? (*c*) How were group members selected in the first place, and how was the group's convener appointed? (*d*) How necessary is the group? That is, to what extent does the group overlap with or displace the authority of established governance processes, and to what effect? Participation, like consultation, is insufficient in and of itself. To stand as true participation and to provide an opportunity for the development of "team thinking" as we defined it in chapter 4, a team (even in the form of a committee or commission) should be able to attend to its own defining. At least, it should have the freedom to engage in redefining (i.e., a form of critique) as it deems necessary.

The Interpretive Work of Team Building

One of the critical aspects of team building is creating a climate that includes all team members regardless of differences among them. We view inclusiveness as an obligation of both the team as a whole, through shared norms, and its individual members, through individual practices. Persons who define themselves as apart from the team are, by definition, also out of synch with the team. That is, by holding themselves apart from their group, they void the possibility of fully joining with it. In chapter 5, for example, we discussed the case of Silver College, where a new vice president held himself apart from his colleagues, resisting their well established, team-oriented approach to leadership. By virtue of his self-imposed separation, he fell out of step with the team and eventually had to leave. Thus, inclusiveness has to work two ways: An established team must try to accept a new member, but the new member, in turn, must accept the reality of the team. While the Silver College team genuinely tried to include the new vice president, he, in effect, excluded them by nullifying the culture they had built.

Few works on leadership or teamwork have addressed the thorny issue of inclusiveness. However, as we examined the fifteen teams participating in this study, we identified a number of hidden dynamics related to gender, race, and power inequity that bore strongly on the question of whether a team was truly inclusive or not. As we noted in discussing the Definer role in chapter 4, we believe that decision-making groups need to be conscious of a natural tendency to gravitate toward those whose voices represent the power norm (e.g., the voices of white males) while ignoring others who depart from the group's dominant orientation or ideology (e.g., women, people of color, and some individuals for whom English is not the native language), especially in the formulation of team agendas.

Rosabeth Moss Kanter (1977) reports that corporate managers typically prefer to hire socially similar subordinates. She views this tendency to conform as a mechanism for coping with uncertainty. Because decision making at top organizational levels is complex, the "best choices" (if such can be said to exist) are rarely visible. At this level, knowledge about cause and effect tends to be flawed, and the information that bears on a problem is often equivocal. Realities such as these highlight the fact that rational decision making is often an illusion. In circumstances such as these, the addition of more unknowns—in the form, for example, of "strangers"—may produce high levels of anxiety. Rosabeth Moss Kanter explains:

> It is the uncertainty quotient in managerial work, as it has come to be defined in the large modern corporation, that causes management to become so socially restricting: to develop tight inner circles excluding social strangers; to keep control in the hands of socially homogeneous peers; to stress conformity and insist upon a diffuse, unbounded loyalty; and to prefer ease of communication and thus social certainty over the strains of dealing with people who are "different." (P. 49)

Kanter (1977) also points out that "people who do not 'fit in' by social characteristics with the homogeneous management group tend to be clustered in those parts of management with least uncertainty" (p. 55). This may contribute to the well-known pattern in higher education of women filling the vice presidency for student affairs rather than the vice presidency for academic affairs or financial management. Presidents tend to give more attention to academics and finances—areas with far more uncertainty than student affairs—and they may instinctively try to fill those positions with people who are like themselves. Of the fifteen teams in our study, four had women in the vice presidency for academic affairs, one woman filled the position of vice president for finance, and two women were in the role of vice president for student affairs. Four teams had women in the presidential role. Of the fifteen teams, six were all men, four had one woman on the team but not as president, and another five had mixed membership (i.e., more than one woman on the team). Four of the five mixed teams were headed by women presidents, indicating that when a woman formed a team she included at least one additional woman as a team member.

Achieving Inclusiveness in Teams

The building of an inclusive team requires *interpretive skill*—the ability to *discern* and *bridge* differences in how people see, understand, and feel about their situations (Chaffee 1984; Neumann 1989; Neumann, in press b). We used the term *Interpreter* to describe one of the core thinking roles in teams. Within the core of team thinking, the Interpreter bridges diverse understandings among people. In this chapter we take this concept further in that we speak of *interpretive skills* as the abilities of people in leadership positions to bridge differences in levels and forms of meaning.

An interpretive president is a thorough observer of what goes on in her or his administrative team. What this means is that an interpretive president is able and actively seeks to discern what is happening within the team in both a *literal* sense and a *figurative or symbolic* sense.

It is important to distinguish between literal interpretation, and figurative or symbolic interpretation. Simply stated, a literal interpretation is a straightforward recording of behaviors and events (e.g., I notice that a team member says little at meetings). A figurative or symbolic interpretation is a meaning attributed to behaviors and events (e.g., I infer that a team member says little because he is not tuned in or because he feels left out). A president (or any team member) who perceives at both levels—who reads simultaneously for the literal meaning of an event and its symbolic meaning—displays interpretive skill.

Let us consider another example, this time of a leader who is quite attuned to the literal dimension of organizational events but overlooks their symbolic undertones: Two colleagues, a woman and a man, arrive at a meeting. The person chairing the meeting greets the woman warmly and comments sincerely, "What a great hat. It makes you look like a model. You remind me of Mata Hari." Then, in a more businesslike tone, the chair turns to the man and says, "Michael, I am glad you were able to make it after all. Your ideas about this new project should really help the group move along quickly."

Without the surrounding noise and activity, and without an appreciation for the rapidity with which the incident occurred, this conversation appears extreme. But have most of us not witnessed or been party to such interactions, occurring so quickly amidst distraction, and in the outer "margins" of main events, that they go by unnoticed? Our tendency is to view such exchanges literally: The chair welcomes the two guests, complimenting the fashionably dressed woman and verbalizing his expectation that the man will make important contributions during the course of the upcoming meeting. However, an interpretive perspective that attends to symbolic as well as literal meanings yields an additional view: the explicit reference to the woman's physical appearance and style of dress reinforces the traditional status of women as objects to be seen and admired but not necessarily heard. This is the symbolic reading. Moreover, what remains unsaid is also of symbolic value. The woman is not associated openly with the activity of intellectual contribution, as the man is. The man is not cast symbolically as a "decoration," as the woman is.

It is difficult to convey this double interpretation to both men and women because we are accustomed to making literal interpretations and giving little attention to coexisting symbolic meanings, even when the symbolism performs the powerful function of defining expectations and status, either in terms of what is said or what remains unsaid. Moreover, because symbolic readings are often difficult, even painful, we may purposefully turn away from them. However, people's symbolic understandings of their own and each other's roles in relation to their group may influence their feelings about whether or not they truly belong to it. In this way, symbolic levels of interpretation may affect just how inclusive a group really is. In the situation cited above, a symbolic analysis leads to the conclusion that the man was welcomed as an intellectual contributor to the meeting. The woman, while greeted with great warmth, was not welcomed in the same way. A team builder who understands events literally and symbolically can see the many ways in which we leave others out of the group process, whether literally or symbolically, and whether intentionally or not.

Why do leaders have such a hard time seeing both the literal and the symbolic dynamics of their teams? Familiarity usually makes it difficult to observe how a group works and how members interact. Processes that appear puzzling to a stranger are taken for granted by persons who have been with the team for a long time because they have adapted to the design of their team reality. For this reason, an interpretive perspective requires that leaders, like anthropologists who study a new culture, "defamiliarize" themselves with customary ways of viewing their group. The leader-as-anthropologist should approach the team's reality on its own terms, almost as if seeing it for the first time. But how would the leader do this?

Linda Smircich tells us that "it is difficult for us, researchers and managers alike, to both live in our cultural context and to question it" (1983,

p. 355). However, in striving for defamiliarization, a leader may also begin to pose critical questions about the taken-for-granted processes that compose the team's reality. Questions such as the following are likely to force a person in the team-building role to look again at a presumed reality:

- What does the group talk about?
- Who in the group talks and who remains silent?
- Who in the group influences what is talked about?
- What seems not to be talked about in group discussions?
- What are the nonverbal means of communicating?

Removing the Blinders of Privilege

Individuals who hold privileged positions in a group—whether by virtue of power, authority, expertise, membership in a dominant coalition, or control over resources—are frequently unable to grasp the subtle ways in which less powerful members are alienated from the group. An illustration of this phenomenon follows.

At a recent meeting of the board of trustees of an educational organization, the sole woman member tried unsuccessfully to put on her name tag. The problem, she quickly realized, was that the name tag was meant to be clipped to a garment that has a pocket—the kind typically worn by men, a shirt or suit jacket. The "gendered" nature of the name tag was invisible to the male trustees; this is not surprising since a name tag is not a particularly noticeable object. The name tag, which had been intended, literally, to facilitate introductions and camaraderie among strangers, assumed a different (that is, symbolic) meaning for the sole woman in the group: It served as a reminder of women's ever-present struggle to establish their names and to be heard, particularly in predominantly male contexts. Had the woman not risked ridicule by forcefully speaking out, "Let us not have these name tags at future meetings; they are made for men," her colleagues would have remained unaware of the name tags' implicit meaning, and of how that meaning made her feel.

Incidents such as this occur all the time. Women, members of underrepresented ethnic groups, and persons for whom English is not the native language are often excluded from discussion, or they are forced into silence by little, and not-so-little, reminders that they are not at the center of their group's discourse. The silencing of these "less privileged" is not always intentional. Certainly, it was not a conscious decision to provide "made-for-men" name tags at the trustee meeting. What is at issue here, and what is of particular relevance in team building, is that the mechanisms of silencing and exclusion usually slip by unnoticed. This is because, as individuals, we typically interpret events on the basis of our singular experiences and understandings. Only rarely are we fully conscious of the fact that what we see, know, and mean is not necessarily shared by others, even those with whom we work closely. The sole woman trustee's interpretation of the name tag was informed by the accumulation of a lifetime of experiences as a member of the "second sex." None of her male colleagues arrived at this interpretation because membership in the "second sex" was never part of their experience. However, despite the inevitability of some "blinders," people—particularly those in privileged positions—can actively try to understand the lived experiences of others.

A concern with inclusiveness can help a president or team builder be more perceptive of relationships within the team: Are team members getting along? Do they work together? Do they compete? Does someone get left out? In asking such questions a team builder can begin to think in terms of building a real and complex team. Team builders who are not oriented toward inclusiveness are unlikely to see the rifts within their teams; they are, therefore, unlikely to do anything about the rifts. The idea of a complex team that acts like a connected "social brain" may be more illusion than reality for them.

In addition, presidents and other team builders have to be particularly careful not to stereotype and delimit women and minority members by expecting them to assume the role of Definer *only* or *always* when the team is dealing with gender or minority-related issues. As we pointed out earlier, the relegation of minority and women's issues solely to female or minority members of the team does not demonstrate true inclusiveness because it often results in women and minority members being left out of the defining role for larger institutional issues. It also tends to define minority and women's issues as the responsibility solely of minorities and women rather than as a shared responsibility of the whole team. Let us consider an example of exclusion from our sample.

The new president of Marble College started his term by putting together a team that had only one woman, a vice president who was "inherited" from the former administration. "We do not have a strong sense of emotional team," she told us. "On second thought, maybe the men have that—a sense of team. It's a male bonding thing and I am not part of that."

We quickly discovered that her feelings were not unfounded. Her male colleagues made it clear to us that this woman vice president was *persona non grata* on the team, and they pushed her away by questioning or actively denigrating her competence. One of the male vice presidents said,

"She and I will never form a team." Another said, "There is a coalescing of the vice presidents with the exception of her." And a third remarked, "She is a weak leader. She is not very well respected. She is not well perceived by the academic community." A fourth vice president noted, "She is a great gal but she does not provide forceful direction." When we turned to the president for his perceptions of team life, he told us, "As far as I know they [the team members] all relate well to one another." When we asked him pointedly, "Are there any sources of conflict in the team?" he responded briskly, "Not that I know of." As this case suggests, a president who neglects to attend to the quality of relationships within the team neglects to build a context within which teamwork, including thinking together, can occur. As a result, it does not.

Although several of the teams included in this study were homogeneous with respect to ethnicity and sex, the team of the future is likely to reflect greater diversity, particularly as increasing numbers of women and people of color assume administrative posts in colleges and universities. In view of this, it is incumbent on presidents and team builders generally to appreciate the diverse interpretations that team members may bring to issues before the team. They should understand that a team member's interpretation of an issue is likely to be influenced not only by the person's position within the group and within the college but also by that person's position in the outside world. What this requires, on the part of the team builder, and also on the part of other team members, is a clear effort to understand how the "other" perceives reality, given that person's unique point of view.

Let us return to the case of Marble College and imagine that, in place of the current president, there is a president who is more interpretive in his thinking about team dynamics. This newer president would likely ask himself: (a) What is it like for the woman vice president to be the only member left over from the previous administration? (b) What does it feel like to be the only woman on an all-male team? We doubt that the real president of Marble College posed such questions, simply because most people rarely question the taken-for-granted aspects of daily life. This is, in fact, a very difficult thing to do. However, we believe that a president's efforts at team building are enhanced by attempts to sense the worldview of others—that is, to "take the role of the other."

Learning to "Take the Role of the Other"

In previous work, we have discussed the importance of presidents being able to "take the role of the other" (Bensimon 1991a), including their need to realize that what they see and experience, from their privileged

positions as institutional heads, is likely to differ dramatically from what
faculty and others, particularly those of lesser status and power, experience (Neumann, in press c). The concept of "taking the role of the
other" refers to a person (in this case, the president) considering a situation, action, or assumption from the perspectives of others. A president
who "takes the role" of an "other" musters feelings of empathy that give
rise to gestures signifying to the "other" that "I am one with you in
spirit" (Bensimon 1991a). A vice president on one of our real and cognitively complex teams provided a good example of this: "When an issue
is raised I try to look at it through the eyes of that person. You have to
realize the person's situation and understand how it affects them."

Although it has a common-sense feel to it, "taking the role of the
other" requires a conscious rethinking of normative conceptions of decision making and problem solving. "Taking the role" of a "particular
other" (Harding 1983) goes against the grain of conventional theories
of administration, which are grounded in the notion of the individual
making decisions independently based on an impersonal judgment of the
facts in relation to abstract principles of morality. From the perspective
of conventional understandings of administration, the individual strives
to "take the role of the generalized other"—in effect, a disembodied,
unreal, abstraction—rather than the real, particular person to whom he
or she is relating at a particular moment (see Harding 1983, Gilligan
1982). Building on Carol Gilligan's studies of differences between wom-
en's and men's moral development (1982), Sandra Harding (1983) differentiates further between "taking the role" of the "particular other" as
opposed to the "generalized other" by proposing two different ways to
view rationality, one typically associated with women, the other with
men:

> A rational person, for women, values highly her abilities to empathize and
> "connect" with particular others and wants to learn more complex and
> satisfying ways to take the role of the particular other in relationships. . . .
> For men, in contrast, a rational person values highly his ability to separate
> himself from others and to make decisions independent of what others
> think—to develop "autonomy." And he wants to learn more complex and
> satisfying ways to take the role of the generalized other. (P. 55)

In sum, "taking the role of the particular other" is an attempt at genuine
understanding of the lived experience of another person, while "taking
the role of the generalized other" represents the abstract conceptuali-
zation of that person's situation as being of "such and such a type"
(Schutz 1967, p. xxv). The distinction between these two forms is that
"taking the role of the particular other" depicts an effort at genuine

understanding of someone else's subjective experience while "taking the role of the generalized other" represents categorization (Schutz 1967) and hence objectification of someone's lived experience.

Even though taking the role of the particular other is associated strongly with how women construct their social world, the ability to take the role of the other should not be viewed as foreign to the experience of men. Nor should men be viewed as unable to learn, from the experience of women, how to interpret and understand the situations and circumstances that affect the lives of others.

A recent book by Deborah Tannen, *You Just Don't Understand: Women and Men in Conversation* (1990), provides numerous lessons on how to "take the role of others." Tannen's point is that women and men talk differently. She characterizes women's discourse as "rapport-talk"— the use of conversation to establish connections and negotiate relationships. She contrasts this with men's discourse, which she describes as "report-talk" because it serves primarily to "preserve independence and negotiate and maintain status in a hierarchical social order," a task that men typically accomplish by "exhibiting knowledge and skill, and by holding center stage through verbal performance such as storytelling, joking, or imparting information" (p. 77). In most public settings, such as professional meetings (except meetings of groups composed only of women), the mode of communication is more like "report-talk" than "rapport-talk"; this poses a disadvantage to women attendees.

Male-female dynamics in groups raise unique challenges. We recently observed an African-American woman make a very perceptive recommendation at a meeting of a policy-making body. Her comment, however, was overlooked, and the discussion moved on to other subjects. A few minutes later, a man restated the point exactly. This time, however, the group picked it up, discussed it at length, and resolved to act on it. The man was praised for his contribution. Several questions came to mind as we observed this situation:

- Why did the group bypass the woman?
- Why did they attend and respond to the man?
- Was the situation idiosyncratic?
- Did anyone else realize what had just taken place?

In response to the first and second questions, Deborah Tannen's work suggests that the group may have ignored the woman's comment because it came from a woman who was also a member of a minority group. When the same point was made later in the meeting by a man who was more representative of majority norms, it was heard. We should note that the woman we are discussing was, at the time of the meeting, the highest ranking female administrator in a major research university. Simply put, given her position in the university and her personal stature, she was not easy to overlook.

Tannen's study also suggests that the group ignored the woman's comment because it did not reflect the more conventional, male-oriented "report-talk" of most professional meetings. That is, the woman made too brief a statement, and she spoke tentatively, presenting her point as a question rather than as a statement of fact. In contrast, the man spoke at much greater length and used language that, according to Tannen's research, is likely to have conveyed "the same idea with a different metamessage: 'This is important. Take note' " (p. 239).

Was this incident idiosyncratic? We think not. Tannen reports that many women have encountered similar situations, but she also says that a similar phenomenon occurs among men who are not adept at "report-talk" or who are unable to frame statements in ways that make them sound important. We pursued the question further by talking with the woman after the meeting. She was, in fact, aware of what had taken place and said that the same thing had happened several times before. She attributed such occurrences to sexism and racism, and indicated that she had not considered that they might also be a function of the "genderedness" of discourse styles. While the woman was aware of what had just happened, we found no other meeting participants, including the man who restated the woman's comment, who were aware of what had transpired.

Some might say that the best way to deal with situations such as this is to learn the dominant discourse. Indeed, this is how most women (and minorities) adapt to public situations. But this is not the only possible response to the problem of insufficient inclusiveness, nor do we view it as a real solution. At this point the notion of "taking the role of the other" becomes particularly instructive. If the chair of the meeting (or, for that matter, any other participant) had been conscious of the ways individuals were being silenced or certain forms of talk ignored, that person would have been in a position to "take the role" of the woman administrator. For example, once the chair, having assumed the role of this woman, recognized the situation the woman was in, he could have refocused the group's attention back onto her. This would likely have entailed picking up on her statement, for example, by affirming it or by outrightly agreeing with it, by adding to it, by asking her to elaborate on her point, or by inviting others to reflect on what she had said. That is, the chair could have made the point that the statement was the woman's—not the man's—originally.

We caution that "taking the role of the other" is not synonymous with taking a protective stance. What may look like a demonstration of support for a less privileged member may be anything but that if the gesture accentuates the "other's" lower status or difference from the norm. We provide this brief example:

A colleague of ours told us that after she made a presentation at a meeting where she was the only female presenter among a group of more seasoned researchers, a person who was familiar with her work took it upon himself to elaborate at great length on her remarks. He informed the group that, among other things, she had underplayed the scope of the work. Even though his action was intended to support and emphasize the uniqueness of her work, it had a very different effect. Our colleague had purposely chosen to make a brief and simple presentation, but the uninvited interjection made her appear incapable of speaking on her own authority. She looked as if she needed to be rescued or protected. As we might expect, the interjection of a more "authoritative" voice deflected attention from her and toward that voice. Had our colleague pointed this out to the well-meaning individual, she might have appeared as overreacting. To call one's co-workers' attention to subtle manifestations of patriarchy, sexism, and racism is to risk greater exclusion.

This is where an interpretive leader who can "take the role of the other" and can respond effectively to thorny situations, such as those of our colleague and the African-American woman, can help. A perceptive and conscientious discussion facilitator who becomes a thorough observer of team interactions—of both their literal and symbolic manifestations—may be able to detect subtle but deeply felt negative messages among team members. By carefully maneuvering a group's conversation, the facilitator may be able to correct such dysfunctions. The facilitator may also be able to educate other team members as to how certain patterns of interaction may ignore important differences among people (e.g., unique viewpoints) while perpetuating differences that are far less important (e.g., status differentials).

Team Building from a Cultural Perspective

What stood out about the illusory or simple teams in our sample was that many of their members complained that their team lacked a sense of purpose. It is not surprising that many saw their team's directionlessness as a reflection of flaws in their president's leadership. Because these complaints occurred so often, we wondered whether the formulation of a clear purpose might not be an essential aspect of team building. We heard about the importance of purpose so often, in fact, that we originally planned to begin this chapter with something like: "The first rule of team building is that the president must establish a sense of direction for the team."

Luckily, in preparing to write, we came across a random note scribbled months back: "Convergence on means is what gives a team direction." This string of words, inspired, we think, by Karl Weick's book, *The Social Psychology of Organizing* (1979), made us realize that the deficiency in teams we had labeled "illusory" and "simple" had little to do with their lack of unified purpose or direction, or with the absence of clear and elevating goals as such. What these teams really missed was the opportunity to experience "convergence." Many of the simple teams were operating in settings that were anything but conducive to a convergence of minds. While they may have *thought* that having goals would provide them with just such an opportunity, previous studies (Birnbaum 1988) have shown that the road to convergence is not likely to be paved with goals. We see it as paved with something different.

Our study leads us to believe that a team's "convergence" arises not from formally established goals but from something far more personal and meaningful—the shared values, respect, concern, and appreciation that we are likely to find in a truly interactive, inclusive team. In brief, while others may call for goals and purposes, we call for convergence that is rooted in connectedness. At the same time, we realize that creating a connected team in which the expressive function helps team cognition come alive takes a good dose of standard administrative and utilitarian work. After all, as we pointed out in earlier chapters, in order to be a team, members have to meet regularly, they need to share in shaping the team's agenda, and their meetings must be more than opportunities for "information delivery." Moreover, real teams must acknowledge and address even the most subtle conflict, and team builders must attend carefully to interactive processes within the group and to members' perceptions and feelings about them.

As we noted in chapter 2, our studies have led us to believe that the conventional athletic-team metaphor is a poor representation of the administrative team. Rather, we have come to view the team as a cultural system. We see culture as a more fitting and more powerful metaphor for the team because it calls attention to "the pattern of symbolic relationships and meaning sustained through the continued processes of human interaction" (Smircich 1983, p. 353). Moreover, the culture metaphor's emphasis on interpretation—on how people make meaning—is consistent with our description, in earlier chapters, of teams as systems of doing and thinking.

The point we make in this chapter is that viewing the team as a culture has implications for how team building should be approached. From a cultural perspective, team building involves understanding groups as socially and psychologically alive—that is, understanding how groups come together and come apart, how they bring in some people and exclude others, and how they make meaning, for example, by invoking symbols of power and privilege. More important, team building, defined culturally, requires a thorough understanding of what individual members see, experience, and feel within their group, and it requires a patient willingness to address group dysfunctions. Team building consists, above all, in shaping meaning in such a way that a group comes to see itself as a team. Thus, relational and interpretive work is the essence of team building, and it is through such work that convergence and connectedness become possible.

In sum, the culture metaphor divests the team of its formalism and portrays it instead as a live human group that is always changing, always in flux, always in the process of becoming. From this perspective, team building involves the giving and sustaining of life within a group rather than the mechanical piecing together and tuning of its physical parts.

7

Reconstructing Collegiate Leadership as a Collective Practice

This chapter addresses the following proposition: Because of their highly differentiated cognitive abilities, the complex (and *real*) teams that we discussed in previous chapters are better able than simple (and illusory) teams to discern the changing needs, positions, aspirations, and particularly points of view of diverse members of the campus community. Due to their complexity, these teams are able to discern and comprehend a variety of messages, at both literal and symbolic levels, and they are in a better position than the simple teams to work with what they hear. In brief, they have a clear advantage in formulating meaningful responses to new and highly diverse campus voices. In this 'sense, complex teams are in an ideal position to guide the rethinking and reshaping of campus realities.

We begin this chapter by examining the nature of change on our campuses. We also try to glimpse the type of leadership that can respond meaningfully to such change. We say "glimpse" because we believe the nature of the new leadership is still being forged on campuses throughout the United States. We then elaborate on why leadership teams that work as cognitively complex social brains, or as cultures, are adept at responding to change. We conclude with some guidelines about the exercise of complex, culturally grounded team leadership in rapidly changing, increasingly diverse campus worlds.

In line with our cultural model, a brief qualification is in order: We are not asserting that teamwork is important because it gives managers power. Ours is different from conventional management theories that advocate teamwork as one more instrumental strategy to gain control over organizational processes. We are instead concerned with making leaders look at and think about the practice of leadership—what they do and do not do, and why, and what these patterns reveal to the leaders themselves about their own values, interests, and commitments. While we urge leaders to reflect on the values and aspirations inscribed within their own practice, we urge them also to reflect on the experience of "the particular other"—of the woman or man who, by virtue of different experience, background, or orientation, stands outside the traditional circle of power but is nonetheless subject to it.

Changing Campus Worlds and Changing Leadership Tasks

American higher education is in flux. Campuses are thrown into dis-equilibrium by new voices in academe, among both the faculty and the administration—people of color, women, lesbians and gay men, people whose social and economic origins would have barred them from American higher education during previous eras, both as students and as professional educators. Colleges nationwide are attempting to make their curricula more encompassing. Many institutions now require undergraduates to fulfill "diversity" requirements, for example, by taking courses on the culture and life of non-Western societies. On campuses throughout the country, there is a call to fulfill what Johnetta Cole, the president of Spelman College, has described as "the promise of diversity."

In one sense, the changes occurring on our campuses are tangible. They come in the form of new courses, programs, academic requirements, and policies reflecting a desire for increased tolerance, if not acceptance, of difference. But in another and more important sense, these changes are intangible, though deeply felt, as they creep into our minds and emotions and force us to come face to face with the ambiguity that arises when our established knowledge, including our long ingrained ways of knowing and being in the world, is shaken. On today's campuses, administration is no longer a matter of "negotiating" concessions to the idiosyncratic concerns of special interest groups clamoring for equal treatment, or, as some would have it, "their piece of the resource pie." Rather, the task of the administrator and any leader today is to discern and to act responsively from an understanding of differences among "a plurality of voices vying for the right to reality—to be accepted as legitimate expressions of the true and good" (Gergen 1991, p. 7). This interpretive task, however, is not one that comes easily, even when we know and openly acknowledge that established ways of thinking are misdirected, incomplete, or simply wrong.

Despite a plethora of works disavowing the romanticized image of the university as a harmonious community of scholars living in a world bound by collegially derived rules and norms (Baldridge 1971; Bensimon, Neumann & Birnbaum 1989), we often fail to think and talk about the anarchic reality behind the idealized images we so ardently disavow as false. Despite our critiques of such images (Baldridge 1982), we hold fast to them—for example, to ideals of what it means to be part of an academic community as a professor, administrator, trustee, and perhaps most important, a student. Entrenched ideas (e.g., collegiality) are hard to change, especially when the alternative view (e.g., the university as an organized anarchy) is negative and conflictual, or absent; we still have very little to replace the ideas that we declare false. Holding on to falsehoods may be easier than admitting to ambiguity.

The dominant image that people typically have of the college or university is of a cohesive whole in which all aspire to the common goal of "true knowledge." While we know better, we rarely acknowledge that the word *student* means different things to different people, that *community* can refer to a group that holds itself apart from the whole, and that *knowledge* (including college-certified knowledge) may lie outside the common ken and may, at times, contradict it. A recent article in the *New York Times* under the headline, "Separate Ethnic Worlds Grow on Campus," exemplifies the ambiguity surrounding what it means to be a college student, not to mention a college graduate, in North America today by describing how students of diverse ethnicities and races are choosing to enact their social and cultural realities on campus. Consider this excerpt: "Sergio Perez lives in an off-campus apartment with other Chicano students at the University of California at Berkeley. A senior, he is majoring in Chicano studies, and participating in bilingual commencement exercises reserved for Chicano and Latino students" (18 May, 1991, p. 1).

In a context such as this, the task of leadership is to come to know the differences in identity and experience that Sergio Perez and his community proclaim, and to foster an environment where those differences can be expressed and can thrive. In sum, the ascendancy of "communities of difference" (Tierney, in press), such as the Chicano and Latino community at Berkeley, highlights the fact that administrators need to consider how their approach to "doing administration" discerns and responds to the changing context of the academy, including changes in the meaning of common words such as *student* and *community*. Regardless of the substance of the administative response, we would view it as incomplete and inadequate if it remained blind to a portion of campus life that is very real to its inhabitants.

Changing Administrative and Leadership
Practices in Changing Campus Worlds

Administrators and other leaders who persist in conventional leadership practices, for example, focusing on the thinking and agenda of just one person or just one type of person, are likely to become less and less effectual as the worlds and realities around them change. One of the points we have made in this book is that the strength of teams lies in their ability to think together in ways that individuals typically cannot do (see chapter 4). We wish to add an important point to this: thinking together means, in part, reflecting together. It means reflecting on individual administrative practices, on team practices, and perhaps most important, on the experiences of others outside the team who must live within the realities defined, at least in part, by administrative leaders—be they the workplace realities of faculty and staff (Austin & Gamson 1983), the resource realities of the institution (Neumann 1990b), or the organizational realities represented by diverse collegiate cultures (Bensimon 1990a). It is important for administrators and other leaders to acquire a multidimensional view of what they are doing, intentionally or not, to others outside their leadership circle.

While reflective leadership sounds appealing, it is extraordinarily difficult to achieve, requiring sustained dialogue among persons whose views may be highly conflictual. Yet it is leadership built on the model of open, reflective, often conflictual dialogue that is essential to increasingly diverse campuses. It is especially important for administrators who are intent on discerning the reality of change in the classrooms, dorms, and campus grounds, and also on responding to change with sensitivity and meaning.

The imperative to reconstruct the meaning and practice of leadership so that it reflects openness to learning and reflection was particularly evident at the 1991 meeting of the American Association for Higher Education, where the changes engulfing college campuses emerged full blown. The conference theme, "Difficult Dialogues," forced into the open hard-hitting discussions of AIDS education, sexual harassment, homophobia and heterosexism, multiculturalism, and a host of topics emphasizing differences—not uniformities, not consistencies—in how diverse groups experience their campuses. The dialogues that took place at the meeting were unlike typical academic discourse: they were tense, emotional, and also highly personal. Most of all, they made the point that colleges and universities are not abstractions. They are real life, created and recreated by those who live within them (Greenfield 1980).

While they reflected the realities of everyday life on college and university campuses, the dialogues at that meeting dealt with those realities more openly, directly, publicly, critically, and at greater length than they typically are addressed on any campus. As the meeting came to an end, Alison Bernstein, associate dean of the faculty at Princeton University and chair of the AAHE Board of Directors, spoke about the meaning the discussion had for her:

> What I am struggling with is how what we've done together here—as perfectly half-empty, half-full as it has been—can have the fullest meaning for us as individuals. How do we translate our experience back to our campuses, to all the different campuses in which we work and live and try to conduct our lives ethically? Can these difficult dialogues that we have simply begun here have their analogs on our own campuses in ways they didn't have before? (1991, p. 9)

As brief as it is, this statement is important for its central question: "Can these difficult dialogues . . . have their analogs on our own campuses in ways they didn't have before?" The question forces us to ask whether conventional conceptions of "good leadership" provide the space needed for administrators and others to engage in truly reflective and probing dialogues such as those that occurred at the AAHE conference. If we interpret the changes currently experienced by higher education through the lens of conventional leadership theory, they look like systemic quirks and dysfunctions. The conventional, functionalist perspective of leadership directs the administrator simply to "figure out what's wrong with the system," usually through legal-rational or political-negotiation means, and to restore it to its former state. While this approach may work in a technical sense, it is likely to suppress the "difficult dialogues" that would question what the system as a whole is doing, how it is doing it, and most important, why. It would, in brief, ignore the question, Why is the system malfunctioning?—a question that would lead us to consider the system's overall form, intent, and utility, in addition to its state of repair.

Recently the case of the Stanford University doctor who resigned a tenured professorship because "she was long subject to demeaning comments and unwelcome advances" from her male colleagues (*New York Times*, 4 June 1991) was much publicized. An administrator guided by conventional leadership theories would probably call for an investigation of the doctor's accusations of sexism, which, if substantiated, would lead to rules and regulations for averting similar incidents. It is not likely that administrators trained to use a conventional, functionalist perspective aimed at preserving the status quo (through repair) would view this incident as an opportunity to reflect on how current administrative policies are working, and more important, on how others—the victimized doctor in particular—experience those policies, for better or for worse. They would probably just conduct a rational analysis of current policies and their "effectiveness" and try to fix or smooth over the quirks in the system that let such a thing as sexism happen.

An administrator whose thinking is largely collectivist, relational, and interpretive would deviate from the conventional view in three important respects. First, we doubt seriously that one administrator would define the problem alone. Rather a team of administrators talking together and to others outside their circle would outline the problem. Second, the team would consider not only the reported deviations from policy (i.e., sexist behavior) but the woman's experience of the context that gives rise to sexism. They would try to understand that context from her point of view. They would, in effect, make every effort to assume the role of this woman as a "particular other" (see chapter 6). In this way, they might come to understand a corner of the university setting in a way they could not have imagined before the incident. Third, they would consider how the context might be reconfigured (not merely repaired) so as to allow people like the female doctor to thrive professionally. And they would be open to the idea of reconfiguration as activity that is far more than structural, legalistic, or policy based. It is likely that reconfiguration, from a revised perspective, would entail changing minds as well as changing policies.

A team is more likely than an individual to view such an incident as an opportunity for true reflection and for concomitant change. Our study suggests that teams that are complex—functionally and cognitively—are more likely to respond to such incidents with sensitivity and understanding than are simple teams, which would likely act to "fix" and "restore" a system rather than question and transform it. Because of their own internal diversity, complex teams are more likely to have someone in their midst who would urge the group to question, in detail, how the university contributes to and condones practices that do harm to individuals and to groups. In the role of Critic, this person could stimulate a team process of questioning how certain university choices and policies affect people, why they are necessary, and how they might be improved.

Teams and groups that think as they act, and that question critically as they think and act, are likely to respond in meaningful ways to the messy and complex problems that always accompany change. In brief, teams that dare to engage in "difficult dialogues," both among themselves and with the campus at large, are more likely to discern and to respond with care and meaning to the changes around them than are teams who respond only mechanically, and in a utilitarian spirit, to quirks that need fixing so that the system can run just as it always has. The team, as we have presented it here, rethinks contexts as much as it thinks about them.

Let us consider another example of how leadership according to our revised view might work in a group or team context. We take the following example from a meeting of the board of trustees of a large public college. The president opened the meeting by proudly presenting a plan to establish an honors program for academically talented students. The president explained to the trustees that program participants would be selected on the basis of their performance on standardized tests. After the presentation, the president opened up the meeting to discussion. Several trustees raised their hands with questions:

> *Trustee A*: What kinds of courses will be offered in the program, and how are these different from the regular curriculum?
>
> *Trustee B*: How many students will participate annually?
>
> *Trustee C*: How much will this program cost us and can we afford it?

After this discussion had continued for a while, Trustee D, rather than asking a question as the others had, offered the following apprehensions:

> Although I am very much in favor of academic programs that encourage specially gifted students, I am opposed to establishing a program whose sole criterion of academic talent is based on test performance. Moreover, I am very concerned that if we approve the program as it has been proposed, minority students, who tend to have lower scores on standardized tests, will be excluded.

Let us consider what happened at this meeting. The president, in laying out the plan that he saw the college pursuing, played the Definer role within the trustee group. He defined what would happen, or in this case, what he wanted to see happen and what he felt *should* happen. Trustees A, B, and C spurred important analytical considerations: Is this program truly different from the regular program, and if so, how? How large will it be? Is it financially viable? In asking these questions—all aimed at filling out the basic information that the president had provided—they took the president's definition (i.e., that an honors program was needed) as a point of departure. Enter trustee D in the role of the group Critic. Trustee D stated his honest reaction to the president's proposal. What was unusual and particularly valuable about his contribution was that it reflected his "taking the role of the particular other"—this time, the minority student who typically experiences standardized tests in very different ways from upper- and middle-class white students and who performs differently on such tests as well. Rather than pondering, as the first three trustees did, how the new honors program would work (and assuming its need as given), trustee D asked himself and his colleagues a more fundamental question—whether the use of standardized tests as the admissions criterion would exclude people in ways they simply should not be excluded. He asked whether the program as defined by the president was, in fact, a good idea.

While we do not know what happened as a result of trustee D's comments, it is clear that, in making his critical statement and in urging the group to engage in a process of critique about a topic obviously dear to the hearts of at least one of its members (the president), he initiated "a difficult dialogue." It is deliberations of this sort that we believe are necessary in the face of far-reaching campus change. It is deliberations of this sort that are unique to teams that think, reflect, critique, and rethink together.

But what does it take to develop this kind of team? We suggest four leadership capabilities that are essential to team thinking as we have defined it here:

1. *The ability to understand the subjective experience of particular others.* If colleges and universities are to be "communities of difference," it is imperative that administrative leaders hear and make every effort to comprehend the voices of others. What this often requires is recognition that one's position influences what one notices and interprets. That is, a person's interpretations of the lived experiences of an "other" are always framed by the person's own experience and interpretation of reality (Schutz 1967). Just as we act on personal beliefs about "what's out there," we simultaneously ignore what we cannot see; we either neglect it altogether or treat it inappropriately. Members of leadership teams need to examine how their particular positions within the university or college (for example, as top administrators, department chairs, faculty members) influence what they see, whom they speak with, what they regard as legitimate and credible, and what they classify as normal and abnormal.

Katharine Bartlett (1990) writes, "Because knowledge arises within social contexts and in multiple forms, the key to increasing knowledge lies in the effort to extend one's limited perspective" (p. 882). Each team member has to recognize that her or his perspective provides "a source of special knowledge, but a limited knowledge" that can be improved and expanded "by the effort to step beyond it, to understand other perspectives" (p. 882). While we know that it is important for teams to look outward in order to avoid cutting themselves off from changes outside themselves (note the special contributions of the Interpreter and

Disparity Monitor), we also know that they need to turn inward to consider how their internal processes may facilitate or inhibit the team's individual members from expressing divergent viewpoints: Do members feel free to play the role of Critic? Why or why not? What is the experience of people who try out the Critic role? We found that on several teams this type of introspective consideration was stimulated by people in the Emotional Monitor role, a role that seemed prominent in some new teams but could dissipate quickly.

Without acceptance, understanding, and appreciation, the Critic role also can disappear. We believe it particularly important for presidents, vice presidents, deans, or other persons in team-building roles to invite team members to disagree and challenge their viewpoint. Unless there is a felt sense of permission to critique—to resist uncritical conformity, passivity, and groupthink (Janis 1972)—team members may be reluctant to voice divergent views, to say things that no one else can or will say, to question the seemingly obvious, to disagree with the opinions of authorities, to point out inconsistencies in what is espoused and what is actually done.

2. *The ability to share and interact.* Organizing for real teamwork requires talk. To turn a loosely gathered group of people into a real team there must be opportunity for talk. In talk that is meaningful, "domination is absent, reciprocity and cooperation are prominent" (Belenky et al. 1986, p. 146).

As we pointed out in our discussion of life in simple teams (see especially chapter 5), talk cannot happen in the absence of regularly scheduled meetings. We believe it is the lead administrator's or team convener's responsibility to schedule such meetings and to treat them as sacred. Presidents who often cancel or reschedule cabinet meetings, for example, without regard for the commitments of other team members, present themselves as devaluing and disrespecting their teams. They give off the message that getting together is unimportant in comparison to other tasks. Because building real teamwork takes time together, the lack of time together can create simple teams. It can turn teams into illusions.

Opportunities for continuing interaction are important. The team builder, however, must be especially aware of the ways in which the structure and process of the team, including the behavior of its individual members, may control or inhibit the flow of talk within the team. As we noted in the discussion of simple (i.e., illusory) teams in chapters 5 and 6, inhibition and excessive control of talk and thought on teams can be shown in many ways: through team members' intolerance of diverse viewpoints, through the team's rigid adherence to agendas brimming with administrative minutiae but barren of substance, through the convener's disapproving facial expressions, through team members' communication of mistrust. Team builders need to be especially sensitive to the variety of gestures—conscious or unconscious—that exclude those who do not fit the team's dominant approach to making sense of the life of their organization.

3. The ability to be critical. Difficult dialogues such as those that took place at the 1991 AAHE meeting are accomplished by teams that think and act from critical consciousness (Freire 1984). Such teams are concerned with more than mere organizational function; they are concerned with what their larger organizations stand for and what they enact purposely or inadvertently, openly or in silence. These teams are more concerned about the values and meanings inscribed in their organizational systems than they are about efficiency. And they are concerned with how diverse constituencies experience their organizational worlds rather than only with how to make those worlds work harder, faster, or more productively.

Dialogues that center on critical consciousness emerge only when a team begins to ponder why it is that an accomplished, long-time, tenured faculty member should want to give up a prestigious position in one of the top medical schools in the country, as did the Stanford professor. Dialogues of this sort begin when a team not only calls for an investigation of a specific incident, but also admits, "This incident—what it means and what it may represent—is something we need to talk about," and when it asks: "What is it about the way that we do business (including what we do and what we don't do)—what is it about the place we've created here—that exposes a professor to such infringements and violations? What do people like her see, feel, and experience in their workplaces, in their specific positions, that we, by virtue of our removed positions, may not see, feel, or otherwise apprehend? What might this incident tell us about what life is really like on campus?"

In asking questions such as these, administrative groups can begin to examine how they, as dominant powerbrokers, may participate in creating conditions that marginalize others (Giroux 1990). It is questions such as these, asked often and pondered intently, that initiate and sustain difficult dialogues.

4. The ability to reflect and to learn through reflection. What does it take to turn "difficult dialogue" into a team habit? The work of Donald Schon on how managers learn by reflecting on their actions is insightful. John Smyth (1989) explains Schon's work as follows: "By reflecting upon action, Schon (1983) claims that individuals and communities acquire knowledge, skills, and concepts that empower them to remake, and if necessary reorder, the world in which they live" (p. 196).

During our interviews on fifteen campuses, we noted that few team members thought of their team meetings as opportunities to reflect on what they do, see, and experience in the course of their daily work. Fewer still made conscious efforts to learn from patterns that they made out in retrospect. Consider this example drawn from our study: Asked to describe a critical incident that their team handled collectively, the members of a team told us that they had recently had to deal with the sudden appearance of racist literature on their campus. One by one, team members related their version of what had happened, including how the team responded and with what effect. That was where their stories ended. Despite our probes into the process of their decision making, no one described the team as self-conscious of its process—that is, as thinking together about the quality and direction of the team's collective thinking.

Moreover, we heard no talk about the incident in context. No one asked whether the occurrence was an isolated case, an aberration, or whether it signaled a more serious, widespread pattern. However, this team, as many others would have, treated the incident as a discrete decision-making and action event. They were intent on fixing a truly serious problem, but in their urgency, they neglected to ask whether the problem might not represent a silent and troubled underside to their college. No one asked: What gave rise to the incident, and what does it tell us about the nature of what we are as an organization? This is a question that is much more difficult and important than the obvious, administrative question: How do we resolve this particular problem? How do we fix it so we can go back to the way we were before it happened?

In addition to reporting what we found among the fifteen teams in our study, we refer briefly to what we did not find. The teams in our study did not reflect the learning commonly associated with reflection-in-action (Schon 1983). That is, we found few instances of teams (or individuals) asking themselves questions such as the following:

- Did members of our team have a shared understanding of a certain situation that we faced together? How did we differ in our views? Did we make our differences known to each other?
- How did we frame the problem? What led us to this particular formulation? Was it adequate, appropriate, helpful? Should we have tried a different angle? How might that have been formulated?

- What prompted us to ask the questions we asked? What questions or issues did we avoid? Was this appropriate?
- What might we learn from this experience?

Nor did many teams describe themselves as engaged in directed learning—for example, considering how a particular commentary on the state of higher education, or a new theory about learning, or an incident at another campus, might shed light on particular practices and policies on their campus. The failure to take advantage of opportunities for reflection and for directed learning leads us to believe that the possibilities for "difficult dialogues" within campus teams are severely limited.

Teams are often so caught up in responding to the changes around them that they neglect to question the nature, sources, and deeper meanings of those changes. Teams typically resist the chaos of large-scale change, opting instead for quick opportunities to fix what seems to be broken so that the "system" can resume its former functions. To ask the deeper questions would require opening the door to disorder, argument, differences, beginnings without ends. Such questions would show us what we do not know about our problematic world rather than pointing to clearly demarcated problems. They would open the door to discussions that are frustratingly circuitous and painfully tortuous in their inconclusiveness.

In the face of uncertainty, administrators generally prefer to address problems from policy, financial, or administrative perspectives (as did most of the trustees in the illustration earlier in this chapter). The unspoken rule, when administrators are harried, is to refrain from digging too deeply—to avoid muddying what, on the surface, looks fairly straightforward. It is the person who assumes the role of Critic who is likely to break the imposed peace and to push the team into uncomfortable learning. Teams that value learning—however painful—will protect and value their Critic. But teams that purposefully evade uncertainty are likely to shun and discredit the Critic, and perhaps to drive this person away.

Changes in Leaders' Personal Theories about Leadership

As we noted in chapter 1, institutional leaders, including presidents, have ideologies that frame their definitions of administration and leadership. These ideologies represent *implicit or personal theories* of leadership and organizational life (Neumann & Bensimon 1990). Personal theories are important because they provide team builders with ideal images of leadership teams—what they look like, how they are composed, how they act. A personal theory defines what the concept, *team*, means to a team builder.

Let us consider the case of a team builder who works from a personal theory that is individualistic and functionalist. This person likely thinks of herself as the team's leader and as its hierarchically superior head. She may also see the team as an instrument for monitoring and directing institutional operations. A team builder working from a functionalist theory would define the team as an object for meeting her own individually defined ends because, according to her view of the organizational world, only she can provide leadership. From this perspective, the individual leader, as director of the team, is empowered. The team, however, is passive, even inert.

The team builder who works from a personal theory that defines leadership as a collective and shared activity is more sensitive to the cognitive and reflective potential that resides in the team. Because this team builder defines leadership as a shared, interactive process (rather than a trait, talent, or right lodged in just one person), there is greater equality between the team builder and other members of the team. When status differences are minimized, or openly acknowledged and dealt with, there is less need for self-protective behaviors, and more energy is available for thinking and reflecting. The team builder who works from the personal theory that the team is a structure for dialogue and reflection is not reluctant to give up control of the team's thinking, even if the thinking of others differs from his own views. From a collectivist standpoint, the team is as active in its thinking and its physical behaviors as the team builder.

Team builders need to question their personal theories of leadership, as well as those of other team members, since these theories can and do get in the way of critical dialogue. Personal theories do much more than provide solutions to problems "out there." They formulate—even invent—those problems. Thus, the team builder's (or another person's) implicit theories may create the very problems that the team tries to resolve. Karl Weick's (1979) observation that "organizations paint their own scenery, observe it through binoculars, and try to find a path through the landscape" (p. 136) calls attention to the idea that teams create much of what they see, and that it is, therefore, important to grasp the content, propensities, and biases inherent in the lenses that team members use to make sense of their world.

Summary

Teams that depend on just one person's view of reality have limited ability to discern the complexity of organizational life "out there," particularly during times of change, when established patterns of meaning dissolve. These teams, dominated by solo leaders, therefore have limited ability to respond to change in meaningful ways. Their repertoire of responses reflects only the abilities of the person "in charge." These are, essentially, simple teams. Their claims to teamwork are illusory.

Teams that are more open and equalized in their conception of leadership, that view leadership as a shared process and a shared responsibility rather than as the property of just one person, are generally more effective at discerning the viewpoints, beliefs, and understandings of others. Because these teams see, sense, and think more complexly (i.e., everyone thinks, not just the leader), they are more adept at discerning complexity in their environments. While the responses of a complex team may be slower in coming (because complexity involves more talking and thinking) than the responses of a simple team dominated by just one person, when they finally get played out, they are likely to be more meaningful. The differences between the one-person model of leadership and the model of leadership as shared is captured in the following quotation from Linda Smircich and Gareth Morgan (1982):

> In situations characterized by hierarchical dependency, those in leadership roles are obliged to interpret and assimilate all that there is to observe and understand about a situation before initiating the action of others. In situations of more equalized power, this obligation and ability is more widely spread. Members of a situation are unable to look to authority relations to solve problems; adaptive capacities have to be developed at the level at which they are needed, increasing the learning capacity and adaptive ability of the whole. (Pp. 271–72)

We close this chapter with the following conclusion: complex, team-centered leadership is likely to be more effective than one-person leadership because it demands shared responsibility for thinking as much as it requires shared responsibility for doing. In this way, team-centered leadership enhances the whole team's learning. It also enhances the team's engagement with the life of the campus.

8

Toward the Creation of Teams That Lead, Act, and Think Together

The challenge for the college president, vice president, dean, department chair, faculty member, or trustee who assumes team-building responsibilities is to mold a group of people so that they lead, act, and think together. While we believe that team building is a shared activity and responsibility, we single out, for this chapter, the unique role of the team builder or team initiator—the person who, by virtue of her or his bureaucratically ordained authority, decides to work within a team leadership design, as opposed to a conventional, individual-centered leadership model. We begin with the premise that the very act of initiating a team places certain powers and responsibilities in the hands of the team builder. It is these powers and responsibilities to which we now turn as we proffer advice to people concerned with building the kinds of teams we described in earlier chapters—teams that think and act together; that see and sense, analyze and project, critique and reformulate; that strain to listen and understand inclusively; that reflect, in a critical spirit, on the work of their own hands. The following guide to a team self-study offers suggestions to teams that want to improve their understanding of their work together.

Team Self-Study

An important step in shaping teams that lead, think, and act together involves asking "why things are the way they are, how they got that way, and what set of conditions are supporting the processes that maintain them" (Simon 1984, cited in Smyth, 1989, p. 192). We can begin to address such questions by unearthing *how a particular team is produced*.

In conducting a self-study, we turn the team's structure and process into a problem in need of concentrated examination (Freire 1984). A self-study explores how a team becomes a team, including the variety of factors (both positive and negative) that bring it together and that make it come apart.

Stages of Team Self-Study

A team self-study involves close and careful introspection by the team of its own life patterns. As we define it, the self-study is an examination of the team as a cultural entity. It does not typically happen quickly or easily, nor are its results always readily apparent or immediately implementable. How a self-study happens may be just as important as what comes out of it, and most of the time the self-study process and outcome may overlap dramatically. For example, the way in which a self-study is conducted may serve as a contrast to the way the team typically does its work, thereby giving team members an opportunity to question their standard work practices. Or a self-study, if it "comes off" well, may actually serve as a model for the team's regular process. Because we deem the practice of self-study to be important, we discuss it in detail in its various stages: identifying basic information, collecting the information, dealing with resistance to self-study, scheduling a self-study retreat or meeting, focusing discussion at the retreat, and following up.

IDENTIFYING BASIC INFORMATION

The most important aspect of a self-study is information collection. In our view, key information falls into three parts:

1. information on how the team builder sees her or his role, responsibilities, and accomplishments
2. information on how other team members see and understand the team builder and how they feel about that person's undertakings and presence within the team
3. information on how the team sees itself—how members perceive the group's doing, thinking, and leading together—in brief, the team's self-created culture

In this section we define these three forms of information. In the next section we offer advice on how to collect it and how to use it to increase the team's self-understanding.

Phase 1: How the team builder sees her- or himself. One of our major purposes has been to differentiate functionally simple teams focusing mostly on utilitarian aims to the exclusion of emotion and thought from functionally diverse, complex, and flexible teams. We have come to see the simple team as a somewhat illusory team in that its team builder often speaks quite highly about it while its members question that it functions as a team. On the other hand, we have come to see the complex team as more real in that we found more support, among team members, for what the builders of complex teams said their teams were doing. As this suggests, it is often very difficult for team builders to know whether their teams are working as real teams or illusory ones. To prompt an assessment, we suggest that team builders ask themselves the following questions:

- What is my personal theory of team leadership? That is, why do I have a team? Why do I want or need one?
- Personal theory aside, what does my team actually do as far as I can see? How would I classify my team in terms of its functions? That is, would I categorize the team's work as utilitarian, expressive, or cognitive?
- How does my personal theory of team leadership line up with my observations of what my team actually does?
- What issues do I bring to the team? What issues do I tend not to bring to the team? What is my reason for bringing forth the things that I "put on the table"? What is my thinking with regard to issues I withhold?
- What kinds of things do I reserve for one-to-one discussions with team members? Do I meet with some members more frequently than others? Why? What do the members whom I see less often have in common? What do the members whom I see more frequently have in common?
- Who participates with me in setting the agenda? How does this happen? Who generally does not participate in agenda setting, and why? What sorts of issues typically get discussed? What sorts of issues are reserved for the "tail end" of the typical meeting agenda? What issues do we typically "not get around to"?
- What other patterns are evident in the dynamics of our meetings? For example, whom do I typically look at when I speak? Whom do I avoid? Who looks at me? When others speak, whom do they address—the entire group, me, others in the group? Do I listen to certain persons more than others? When do I typically cut off discussion? When do I get impatient?
- Do I ever discuss with team members how a certain meeting went? Do

I discuss this with certain people and not with others? Why? What do I learn? What may I be neglecting to learn?

Phase 2: How the team sees the team builder. While it is extremely difficult to grasp how others interpret situations and how their interpretations differ from our own, it is even more challenging to apprehend how others see *us*. Alfred Schutz's observation that "No man can see himself in action, any more than he can know the 'style' of his own personality" (1967) points to the need for team builders to probe with care into how others perceive and experience their leadership. This kind of self-reflective knowledge cannot be acquired on one's own because its source resides in the minds of others.

Such knowledge is important because team builders need to know how others feel about them as leaders in order to hypothesize how their style facilitates or inhibits teamwork. Such information can be collected in diverse ways—for example, through third-party interviews, sustained observation, or casual conversation. Team builders, or third-party consultants, can use the following questions to guide their research:

- How do team members feel about the way I communicate, make decisions, involve others in decision making, designate responsibilities, structure agendas? How do they see and feel about the way I interact with them and others one to one and in a group?
- Do the members of my team see me in a consistent way, or are there differences among them in how they construe me as a person and as a leader? What accounts for any differences?
- How do team members describe me in relation to the operating style of the team? How do they evaluate my strengths and weaknesses within the team? What do they see as missing that they think I could provide? To what extent are team members' perceptions of the team's operating style congruent with my own?
- What expectations do team members think I have of them? How do they feel about those expectations? To what extent do they believe that I support their learning—on their own, with others, and with me? How do they think I feel about the mistakes they make and about their shortcomings generally? What do they think of the mistakes I make? How do they assess my desire and ability to learn?

Phase 3: How the team sees itself. Renato Rosaldo (1989) says that "no analysis of human action is complete unless it attends to people's own notions of what they are doing" (p. 103). We suggest the following

questions as a guide to examining how team members make sense of
their work, including how they evaluate it:

- Do members of the team perceive conflict or tension within the team?
  To what extent do team members share in this view? How do they see
  the team addressing this issue? How do they see the team builder's
  involvement in it?
- How do team members describe the work of the team? Do they describe
  teamwork in terms of one or more of the team functions—utilitarian,
  expressive, or cognitive? Are there differences in how team members
  construe the team's functions? Why?
- Which thinking roles are manifest in the team? How effectively are the
  roles played (i.e., does the Analyst inspire a team process of analysis)?
  Who typically plays each role? If any of the roles are missing, should
  they be added?
- To what extent has the team changed over time in relation to who
  plays which thinking role? Are people on the team learning new thinking roles? Are they at least trying them out? If certain roles are reserved
  for certain people, why?
- To what extent is the Definer role shared? What patterns of defining
  are evident on the team? If defining in certain areas is not shared, why?
  With what effects?
- To what extent does the team support and protect the Critic's prerog-
  ative to speak on difficult issues? To what extent is the Critic role
  shared? If it is not shared, is the team tolerant of criticism? How does
  it regard the person in the Critic role?
- Do team members perceive that certain thinking roles are silenced?
  How? Why?
- How often and to what extent does the team talk about its own process?
  Is discussion of process incorporated into the agenda?
- What could individual team members do to strengthen the team? What
  could the team builder, in particular, do?

COLLECTING THE INFORMATION

The second and third sets of information—how team members see the
team builder and how they see the work of the team as a whole—are
particularly sensitive. Who should collect this information, and how? As
we have noted already, team builders, by virtue of their legitimate power,
are in an awkward position; in some respects they are simultaneously
the researchers (or at least, the initiators of research) and the researched.
How direct and open are most team members with the person who

brought them into the job in the first place? Even in the most harmonious of teams, sensitive issues, if brought into the open, may offend to the point of doing more harm than good.

Given the difficulty of collecting sensitive information, we present here three different approaches, which may be used singly or in combination and which should be tailored to a team's unique character:

1. *A consultant collects the information.* The team might call in a third-party consultant to conduct interviews with the leading team administrator (e.g., the president in a presidential team) and individual team members, and also to observe the team in action. Does your team need a consultant? Consider the questions William G. Dyer suggests that team builders ask:*

Do I feel comfortable in trying out something new and different with the team?

Will members of the team speak up and give honest data?

Does the team generally work together without a lot of conflict or apathy?

Am I reasonably sure that I am not the major source of difficulty?

Is my view of leadership and approach to administration consistent with a team approach?

Do I feel I know enough about team building to begin a team without help?

Would the team feel confident enough to begin a team-program without outside help? (Pp. 45-46)

According to Dyer, if six or more of these questions are answered yes, the team does not need a consultant. If four or more are answered no, the team could use a consultant.

While Dyer's questions are useful, we recommend that teams also consider the following factors: If the members of a team characterize their team as functionally simple (i.e., as exhibiting utilitarian but not cognitive or expressive work dynamics) or as missing any of the five core team roles (Definer, Analyst, Interpreter, Critic, Synthesizer), then it is likely to benefit from consultation, at least initially, in laying the groundwork for team building. Consultation might also be helpful if team mem-

---

*These questions were adapted from a questionnaire developed by William G. Dyer (1987, pp. 45–46) to help managers assess the need for an outside consultant to assist in team building.

bers identify the following patterns in their work together: (1) one or two persons play most of the thinking roles; (2) one person, usually the team builder, plays the Definer role; (3) no one plays the Critic role, or one or two play it poorly, either because they are not skilled in the role or because the institutional culture blocks it. Of course, the abilities of team members to recognize these patterns depends on how well acquainted they are with the ideas in this book. We discuss collective reading as a self-study strategy below.

2. A survey gathers the information. It may also be possible to develop a short survey for team members to complete. The questions (presented above) for examining how teams see themselves might serve as the basis of such a survey.

3. Joint reading and structured discussions can serve as an information-gathering device. Teams might collectively read this book and use it as a stepping-off point for self-examination. Several sessions could be scheduled, with each dedicated to the discussion of a specific topic that is particularly relevant to the team.

For this approach, we recommend the following structure: Each session should be convened by a different team member around a particular team topic. In advance of the meeting, the session leader poses questions based on assigned readings, to which team members respond in writing. Team members submit their responses to the session leader before the meeting date.

Session leaders should understand that they are responsible for compiling the meeting agenda, providing team members with questions, and facilitating the group's discussion. In particular, they need to spend a substantial amount of time before the meeting analyzing team members' responses and framing them for discussion. We present suggestions for how to do this in the next section on the self-study retreat or meeting.

DEALING WITH RESISTANCE TO SELF-STUDY

Regardless of the approach, a team builder should bear in mind that team members need to be consulted about both the type of information to be collected and the means of collecting it. In particular, the team builder should share the following information with other team members: the purposes of the self-study as the team builder sees them, the team builder's reasons for engaging in self-study, and the team builder's hopes for the study. Team members should be able to advise on all features of the self-study. More important, they should feel free and welcome to state their opinions, including their reservations, about the undertaking generally.

Not everyone will support the self-study, and some members may express outright rejection. It is important that they feel free to voice their skepticism and suggest alternative ways of going about the self-study. The team builder must take their comments seriously. Statements of resistance to a self-study, however veiled they may be, say a great deal about the state of life on the team. Dyer (1987) suggests the following reasons why people may resist self-study:

> People feel that if they get into team building there will be a "blood-bath." People will get pushed into confronting others or issues that are very sensitive and things might be said or done that will not only be hurtful to individuals but harmful to the work effort.
>
> People may feel that they will be confronted with their own inadequate performance and they would prefer not to deal with this issue in the total group.
>
> They know what the major problems are in the team (a domineering boss, a personal fight between two members, restrictive policies handed down from above, too much work and too few people) and they can't see how team building is going to help.
>
> There is a lot of work to be done and team building will take away precious time. They can't see that the gain will be worth the time.
>
> They have either experienced a poor team-building effort in the past or have heard horror stories about bad experiences and their fears or fantasies conjure up all kinds of negative consequences. (P. 60)

Unless the team confronts sources of resistance openly before embarking on a self-study, those sources—and not the study itself—will be the focus of the team's attention.

SCHEDULING A SELF-STUDY RETREAT OR MEETING

Regardless of how the team chooses to collect its basic self-study information—whether with the assistance of a third-party consultant or through reading-centered diagnosis and discussion—the team should set aside a special time and place for the event. An off-campus retreat is especially conducive to the kind of focused dialogue associated with self-study.

A retreat should be planned with this guideline in mind: For the retreat as a whole, the Definer, Synthesizer, and Task Monitor roles should be shared by as many team members as possible, even if this means that at times persons in bureaucratically "subordinate" positions will be shaping conversations among their "superiors." The retreat should be planned and conducted collectively, with all team members responsible for portions of it. In particular, all team members should share or take turns in facilitating the group's dialogue. This typically requires members to assume defining, synthesizing, and task-monitoring responsibilities. This recommendation pertains especially to two kinds of team situations: (1) teams in which members complain that one or two individuals dominate discussion so that it is difficult to present opposing views, and (2) teams that typically avoid discussions of substantive topics and focus instead on administrative minutiae. Needless to say, facilitators should be designated well in advance of the retreat so that they have plenty of time to design discussion questions and formats.

If a third-party consultant is brought in, then this person can coordinate the discussion, or the consultant and a member of the team may work together as co-facilitators. The point is that everyone should feel invested in the process and outcomes of the self-study. Above all, team building should not consist of sessions in which team members are cast as passive recipients of information dispensed by an "expert" (Freire 1984).

FOCUSING DISCUSSION AT THE RETREAT

The concerns arising from a team self-study are likely to be very sensitive. This was amply demonstrated in our own interviews as, time after time, we listened to expressions of dissatisfaction—about difficult interpersonal dynamics, annoying behaviors, unregulated competition over turf, status differences, feelings of exclusion. The dilemma for the team engaged in self-study is how to talk about these very real aspects of team life without provoking more resentment and divisiveness than already exists.

Edgar H. Schein (1987) provides several helpful ideas for planning constructive discussions on topics that the team needs to talk about. Borrowing from the results of his extensive research, we suggest that in the initial stage of self-study, while the team is still experimenting with the notion of self-study, the team builder take the lead by focusing conversation on "process." This involves directing team members' attention to *how* things are done rather than to *what* is done or to *who* does what to whom. It means focusing the conversation on how topics are selected for the agenda, and on how the agenda is shaped and reshaped (i.e., how the Definer, Critic, and Disparity Monitor roles are enacted), how the team discusses these topics (i.e., how the roles of Analyst, Interpreter,

Critic, and Emotional Monitor are played out), and how the team achieves resolution (i.e., how the Task Monitor and Synthesizer roles emerge).

Focusing on process, especially in the beginning of the self-study, is likely to suggest directions for further discussion within the group, and at the same time to keep the discussion within manageable bounds. What this means is that rather than starting out by pointing to individuals' specific negative behaviors (e.g., Tom constantly interrupting others, Martha not listening, Terry being overly confrontational), the group facilitator poses open-ended questions about patterns of interaction within the team. But in order to know which questions to pose, the session facilitator must have specific data gathered beforehand from individual team members about what their life on the team is like. This preparatory work is often best done by a third-person consultant because collecting data of a personal nature can compromise a session leader who is also a team member. The point is that the session leader does not use such data explicitly to confront individuals with what they are doing wrong but rather to initiate a group discussion on how the group works together, where it goes wrong and where it goes right.

Here is an example. Assume that the session facilitator learns—from interviews with team members, from their responses to a survey, or from their written reactions to this book—that the president has a habit of making negative facial expressions when he hears something he would prefer not to hear. In other words the president makes snap judgments and doesn't listen or weigh opposing views. Rather than confronting the president about the fact that his facial expressions inhibit communication, the facilitator might raise the issue in a *general* form and pose it as a *question*. For this situation, the facilitator might broach the topic this way: "Sometimes individuals display gestures that give the impression that they are not paying attention to the speaker; for example, they may read while a colleague is talking or have a side conversation with someone else, interrupting the speaker. This can cause communication to break down. Can we talk about ways to deal with situations of this sort?" A session facilitator can learn enough from previously collected data to create guiding questions that probe a problematic issue without throwing accusatory data in people's faces. This approach does not merely deal with the behavioral or concrete manifestation of a problem but has the capacity to explore the knowing and feeling that lie beneath the surface of external appearance, tapping, for example, why people may be acting as they do. Getting a handle on people's underlying concerns and beliefs may be more useful in eliciting change than pointing out patterns of disruptive behavior.

A focus on process also helps identify how a team's mode of operation enables or delimits the utilitarian, expressive, and cognitive aspects of teamwork that we defined in chapter 3—for example, whether it emphasizes one aspect at the expense of the others. The data elicited in the three phases of the team self-study might provide some hints as to how team meetings and the team's working style generally reinforce or weaken the utilitarian, expressive, and cognitive functions. In particular, team members should ask themselves, "How does our way of doing things get in the way of the cognitive function?" They might then consider some alternatives to running team business as usual.

The eight roles presented in chapter 4 can also help frame difficult discussions of process. It may be easier to talk about team issues in terms of roles rather than in terms of specific individuals. For example, the "data" collected through the three phases of the team self-study might reveal that Marilyn and Sam, two team members, typically dominate the group's meetings, pushing their agendas forward while others' concerns fall into the background. It might make more sense to cast this issue in terms of the Definer's role rather than in terms of what Marilyn and Sam typically do. For example, the team facilitator might say something like this: "How we do things depends on who assumes the role of Definer. Could we talk about how we enact this role in our team?" Another approach would involve a broader statement such as this: "The way we do things is typically a function of the roles we play and those we don't play. Could we identify which roles are played on this team and which are missing?" Later in the conversation, the facilitator might ask, "To what extent are we making an effort to share in the Definer role? How might we do this better?" The eight thinking roles provide the facilitator with numerous possibilities for analyzing the data emerging from the team self-study, and also for framing the conversation in ways that avoid personal accusation.

FOLLOWING UP

Because teams, like organizations, are forever in the process of becoming (Greenfield 1980)—that is, constantly making and remaking themselves—the self-study should be treated not as a one-time activity but as a continuing process that is part of the history of the team. While it is important not to forget the outcomes of a self-study, it is also important to continue the process even after a retreat or other self-study meeting comes to a close. Without this kind of follow-up, the team may cease to think, question, and learn and may opt instead only to act. In this way, complexity may revert to simplicity, and real teamwork, which requires cognition, may turn illusory.

To maintain the self-study as an on-going team process, the team leader might periodically schedule assessments of how the team is doing relative to the outcomes of the initial self-study event. A follow-up may consist of a dialogue organized around key questions emerging from the earlier session. Questions may be constructed by the group collectively, with each team member assuming responsibility for facilitating discussion around one question. Some teams may prefer that members write out responses to such questions and share them before the follow-up meeting. Others may prefer to use the questions as a broad outline to guide discussion. What is particularly important to realize is that follow-up sessions are valuable only to the extent that they invite self-disclosure and inspire trust among team members. If individuals feel threatened or guarded, then this kind of activity is not likely to be beneficial.

The Team Builder as Observer of the Team Culture

In addition to initiating a team self-study, the team builder can facilitate the formation of a complex team and the conduct of real teamwork by engaging in disciplined, critical, and regular observation of the team. In keeping with the image of the team as a cultural system, we suggest that the team builder act like an ethnographer, striving to decipher the team's culture by observing the tasks it takes on, the processes by which it accomplishes its tasks, and the interpersonal processes that comprise team life (Schein 1987).

DECIPHERING THE TEAM'S TASK

The team builder should take note of what the group talks about and what it neglects to talk about:

- What items are included in the team's agenda?
- Who contributes items to the agenda, and what kinds of items do different people contribute?
- How might these items be classified? That is, what topics do they represent?
- What topics appear to be left off the team's agenda?

By watching and listening to the team over time, the team builder is likely to identify patterns of thought and interaction that vary in their specific content but cohere in their generalized meaning. The team is likely to gravitate naturally to certain topics and to avoid regularly others that it could address. What do these patterns tell about the team? What effect do they have on the team? What makes the team address a topic that it would normally avoid? What are the effects of venturing beyond the team norm?

DECIPHERING THE TEAM'S PROCESS

Task process refers to "the way in which the group works, how it solves problems, gathers information, makes decisions, and so on" (Schein 1987, p. 42). Edgar H. Schein tells us:

> Task processes are elusive. It is easy to experience and to observe them but hard to define and clearly segregate them from the content that is being worked on. Group members learn that they can partially control the content outcomes by controlling the process, as senators do when they filibuster or as debaters do when they destroy an opponent's argument or composure by ridicule, changing the subject, or in other ways diverting the process from what has been said. (P. 42)

Our research showed that not all groups work in the same way. Some of the leadership teams in our study relied on consensus decision making, others voted, and others still turned the final decision over to the president or other administrator. We found that the extent of a team's complexity—the extent to which it engaged in real teamwork—could be discerned through its task processes. Some questions that might help a team builder better understand the nature of the team's process are:

- How do people communicate with one another on the team?
- Do people seem to listen to one another?
- Which of the thinking roles are in evidence and which are missing?
- How can the group's process be understood in relation to the utilitarian, expressive, and cognitive functions of the group?
- How does the group resolve disagreements?

DECIPHERING PATTERNS OF INTERACTION
WITHIN THE TEAM

How team members relate to one another, how they interact, shapes the unique pattern of a team's leading, thinking, and acting together. A team builder intent on understanding the group's interpersonal processes might use the following questions as an observational guide:

- Do team members speak regularly within the group, especially at meetings? Do they listen to each other? Who typically listens? Who does not listen? Who has the ear of most team members? Who is typically ignored or otherwise excluded?

- To what extent do team members talk to each other outside formal meetings?
- What factors facilitate openness (e.g., the feeling that members can ask clarifying questions)? What factors inhibit participation and discussion (e.g., the feeling that members are being scrutinized or judged)?
- Do team members behave in ways that demonstrate respect and caring for one another?

We would urge the team builder endeavoring to decipher the team to be particularly cognizant of the details of team life, including the language that team members use in specific situations, the rituals of team meetings, the forms of nonverbal communication during meetings or other formal exchanges, and patterns of conversation both within the team and, to the extent that it is possible to determine, outside the team. We also encourage team builders, and interested team members, to record their observations of the team in a personal journal and to reread the journal regularly. A journal can assist in identifying patterns of team life and can thereby help a team builder see and capitalize on opportunities for change. A journal provides an opportunity to jot down hypotheses about what the group is doing and why, or what might make the group work in different ways.

Other Thoughts to Bear in Mind

To create a team that leads, acts, and thinks together team builders should bear the following thoughts in mind:

INVOLVE THE TEAM

Teamwork is a collective act, and regardless of how committed a team builder may be to a team's success, real teamwork may not materialize at all if the team is not an active partner in its own development. Involvement means that team members actively participate in formulating agendas, structuring meetings, designing retreats, identifying consultants, and selecting colleagues.

Participation in selecting team colleagues is critical. Members of the team should have the opportunity to meet with candidates who would sit on the team and to influence the selection process. An important criterion in the review of job applicants is simply one of fit. Team members should be able to raise questions such as these as part of the applicant review process:

- How will this person fit in the team?

- Is this person oriented to the idea of a team that does more than simply carry out tasks (utilitarian function)? Is this person oriented to the idea of a team that thinks together (cognitive function) and that supports others in their doing and their thinking (expressive function)?
- Given what we know about this person, which thinking role(s) is she or he likely to play on the team? That is, which thinking process(es) will she or he likely elicit (e.g., definition, analysis, interpretation, etc.)? To what extent is this person likely to participate in team processes initiated by other team members playing other roles? How tolerant is this person of cognitive diversity? How interested is she or he in it? Does this person listen to—and hear—others? How open is this person to learning?
- How comfortable is this person with our mode of operation, with our way of thinking, talking, and acting together?
- How sensitive is this person to dynamics of inclusion and exclusion? What is he or she likely to do about exclusionary dynamics when they happen?
- Would this person be able and willing to reflect on her or his contributions to the team and on the team's workings overall? Would the person be interested in this kind of reflection?

BEWARE OF THE ISOLATING TENDENCIES OF TEAMS

A team is essentially an "observer community" engaged in constructing interpretations of reality (Cooper & Burrell 1988). In our study we encountered teams that were so cohesive—so "together" in a manner of speaking—that their interpretations of reality were at great variance with those of others on campus. These teams had distanced themselves from the rest of the campus to the point of being out of touch with the altogether different understandings of campus reality that faculty and students, and at times even trustees had. Moreover, these teams made no allowances for deviant information; in brief, they had silenced any Disparity Monitors among them.

A team that is in touch only with its own vision of reality and shuts out even the suggestion that there might be other ways to make sense of campus issues is not likely to provide effective leadership. One way to deal with the tendency of some teams to turn too much into themselves is to invite faculty and students to meet with the team periodically. Such meetings should consist of dialogue that flows from a jointly prepared agenda.

STRIVE FOR AUTHENTIC COLLABORATION, BUT DO NOT
BECOME ENAMORED OF ITS POPULARIZED IMAGE

Teams are collaborative units. The best teams that we found in our study were composed of people who "came at things" very differently, as evidenced, for example, by the diverse thinking roles that they played on teams. But rather than flaring into conflict as a result of their differences (though sometimes this could not be avoided), these teams turned the conflictual edge of difference into a constructive edge: their conflict turned into complementarity. We believe that complementarity is at the center of truly collaborative teamwork, for it strives actively to find differences (not similarities) among people and to bring them fully into play. Complementarity demands appreciation and tolerance of difference. It requires a desire to decipher difference, to embrace difference without obliterating it, and simply to learn something new. It requires the coexistence of multiple, simultaneous differences, and it requires active support for the enactment of those differences. This is what we mean by authentic collaboration.

What this implies, however, is that collaboration is not all that, in the popular literature, it is "cracked up to be." Collaboration, like nearly every aspect of organizational life, has its dark side. For one thing, without acknowledging the differences at its core, collaboration is virtually an illusion. Moreover, it is not for everyone. Nor do we believe that people gathered randomly can engage in true collaborative effort. This is why we urge search committees to include team members in the evaluation of job applicants who will sit on a particular team.

Nor do we believe that all collaborative efforts are liberating or empowering. Collaboration that takes unquestioned consensus or uncritical adherence as its core, with little attention to voices that question or that speak to difference, can silence and bow a critical and creative spirit. Or it can turn away the person who would dare to speak up, engendering an ethic that excludes the unique point of view. Moreover, without attending to difference, collaboration can degenerate into groupthink (Janis 1972). While some collaborative efforts may be staged, we believe that collaboration is likely to be best when it rises from within—when people see in each other something that they want to learn, gain, and share. Legislated or mandated collaboration, on the other hand, is often hard to live with and hard to live by. Finally, collaboration without complementarity and without integral meaning may be an empty word, representing appearance more than reality.

Despite its dark side, collaboration—defined as complementarity, as a valuing of differences, as a desire to learn and to connect in difference, and as a natural, personal effort—lies at the heart of real teamwork. It differentiates complexity from fragmentation and from chaos.

EXPERIMENT WITH ALTERNATIVE STRUCTURES AND PROCESSES

While stability has its merits, change can stimulate thinking and learning. Sometimes change can shift a team's approach to leadership altogether. But how can change be engendered in a well-entrenched team? One way to stimulate change is to engage in experiments requiring new, albeit temporary rearrangements (Schein 1987). For example, if the president always sits at the head of the table during team meetings, why not consider rotating the convening function among all team members? If this is a team that is intent on action, why not try something different by initiating a reading and discussion program that involves the entire team? If the team is short of alternative leadership models, why not have the lead administrator observe a colleague in a similar position conduct meetings of her or his group?

Teams and Teamwork: Reality or Illusion?

It has been suggested that teams and teamwork are something of an enigma in that there is little hard evidence to prove that they influence institutional performance, for example, as measured by changes in institutional productivity, financial resources, or quality (Birnbaum, in press). We agree with this position. As long as leadership teams are understood and judged in functionalist terms (do they increase organizational effectiveness and efficiency?), they will, indeed, be a mystery and people will ask, "Why put so much store in something for which we get nothing tangible in return?"

Our response is that what we get *from* teams is not at issue; what we get *through* teams is, and that amounts to the ability of a group of people to think together in more expansive and creative ways than any one person can alone. We do not see the team as the mystery. We see teams as part and parcel of everyday life in organizations. They are familiar, comfortable, natural. As we noted early in this book, we believe that teams are nothing new. They have always been with us. What is unfortunate is that despite their familiarity, teams have rarely been acknowledged. Despite the fact that teams are all around us, we have persisted in living by a myth of solo, all-powerful leadership. It is *this* persistence—

the long-standing, seemingly ineradicable belief in omnipotent, one-person leadership—that stands as a great mystery to us.

We end this book with a question that we did not answer and one that we leave to the philosophers among us: What is it about human nature that has made us believe in solo leadership, in all-powerful individuals, most of whom are males? Why has it been so hard for us to admit to the possibility of the team—to the possibility of connected leadership—especially when we see it around us every day? Why is our language so braced by a vocabulary and syntax that forces our thinking into individualistic lines? We fear that unless we pose these questions as topics for future scholarship, professional discussion, and deep, personal pondering, our argument that teams and teamwork exist and that they can be very real will dissipate.

The attainment of real teamwork requires leadership's best efforts. We say this because teamwork involves attention to processes that many people in leadership positions typically take for granted (e.g., considering patterns of inclusion and exclusion in teams). It also requires a deep commitment to follow through on processes that are hard to grasp and hard to talk about (e.g., relationship building). Real teamwork also requires that people unlearn some of the more sacrosanct definitions of leadership (e.g., leadership as a demonstration of individual heroism) at the same time that they learn new views (leadership as a collective, interactive phenomenon)—in effect, that they reconstruct their well-entrenched learning as they redesign their leadership.

While adherents of individualistic perspectives on leadership may fear that undoing the one-man, heroic myths of conventional leadership theory will also unravel the fabric of organizations as we know it, we believe, with Linda Smircich and Gareth Morgan (1982), that such changes in our thinking will not unravel organizations so much as they will strengthen and democratize them: "Patterns of organization that replace hierarchical leadership with patterns of more equalized interaction in which each has an obligation to define what is happening, and respond accordingly, change the very basis of organization" (Smircich & Morgan 1982, p. 271). What we propose in this book is not the undoing of leadership as we know it so much as its revision and redesign. We offer here more than the typical critique—for example, that one-person leadership doesn't work. We offer, in addition, a replacement for the conventional model—a redesign of leadership as collective, shared, interactive, dialogic, critical, and engaged—and numerous suggestions for how to conceive of leadership in this way and how to bring it into being.

As we have said before, none of this is terribly new. We believe that teams have been with us all along, even before the formation of the modern complex organization. We believe that it is time for us to rediscover teams, to bring them to light, and to revise our conceptions of leadership to make them consistent with the reality of teams.

Appendix A

Sample Interview Protocol

Name:

Title:

Institution:

Date:

Interviewer:

7.0. *Leader Behavior and Interaction*

7.1.   I'd like to switch gears slightly now. One of our interests is to identify how [c] [u] presidents build their administrative teams and work with them. We define the administrative team as the president's inner circle, or as the individuals with whom the president works most closely.
7.1.1.   Who are the members of your administrative team? [Probe: Are there others with whom you work closely?]
7.1.2.   How were these members selected? [Which ones did you select, and which ones did you inherit?]

7.2.   What would you say are the most important functions of an administrative team?
7.2.1.   In what ways do you find the administrative team to be most useful? Least useful?

7.3.   Most administrative teams develop a pattern of behavior or a way of doing business. Sometimes we refer to this as the group's operating style. Could you describe the most important aspects of the administrative team's operating style here at [inst]?
7.3.1.   What roles does _____play? [Ask for applicable individuals.]
7.3.2.   What role do you play within the team?

7.3.3.   How often does the team meet as a group and for what purposes?

7.4.   We've been talking about the idea of an administrative team. To what extent are the _____(#) of you a team?
What do you think most contributed to the making of the administrative team here at [inst]? That is, what did it take to make a team out of several separate individuals?
7.4.1.   What advice would you give to a new college president who has just hired [his/her] executive officers but who has not yet turned them into a team? That is, how should the president go about making a team out of them?

7.5.   I would like to learn a little more about how the team works by asking you to think of a recent, important issue that the team had to deal with.
7.5.1.   Could you tell me what it was about, and how the team handled it?
7.5.2.   Were you satisfied with the team's performance? [Why? Why not? What would you have preferred?]

7.6.   From your experience, what kinds of things should the members of an administrative team have in common? [What makes you say that?]
7.6.1.   How should members of the team differ from each other? [What makes you say that?]

7.7.   [*Optional*] If a newcomer to the administrative team were to ask you, "What are the unwritten rules for the administrative team here at [inst]—the unspoken things I really need to know to get along and to be effective in the team?" what would you say?

7.8.   How would you describe your relationship with the team?

7.9.   Are there any sources of conflict, or tension, within the team?
7.9.1.   How do you deal with them?

7.10.   How would you assess the overall effectiveness of the administrative team here at [inst]?

7.11.   What do you think needs to be done to improve the functioning of the administrative team?

Appendix B

Cognitive and Functional Complexity of Sample Teams

		Cognitively	
		Complex	Simple
Functionally	Complex	5	1
	Simple	2	5

Not classified: 2

Sample total: 15

Definitions:

Functionally complex teams possess all three team functions (utilitarian, expressive, cognitive).
Functionally simple teams lack the cognitive function and usually exhibit only the utilitarian. (See chapter 3.)

Cognitively complex teams possess at least four of the five core cognitive roles (Definer, Analyst, Interpreter, Critic, Synthesizer).
Cognitively simple teams usually lack two or more of the five core cognitive roles. (See chapter 4.)

Explanation:

Chapter 5 compares the functionally and cognitively complex teams to the functionally and cognitively simple teams.

References

Allison, G.T. (1971). *Essence of Decision: Explaining the Cuban Missile Crisis.* Boston: Little, Brown.

Austin, A.E. & Gamson, Z.F. (1983). *Academic Workplace: New Demands, Heightened Tensions.* ASHE-ERIC Higher Education Research Report No. 10. Washington, D.C.: Association for the Study of Higher Education.

Baldridge, J.V. (1971). *Power and Conflict in the University.* New York: John Wiley & Sons.

Baldridge, J.V. (1982). Shared governance: A fable about the lost magic kingdom. *Academe* 68:12–15.

Baldridge, J.V.; Curtis, D.V.; Ecker, G. & Reiley, G.L. (1978). *Policy Making and Effective Leadership: A National Study of Academic Management.* San Francisco: Jossey-Bass.

Bartlett, K.T. (1990). Feminist legal methods. *Harvard Law Review* 103:829–88.

Belenky, M.F.; Clinchy, B.; Goldberger, N. & Tarule, J. (1986). *Women's Ways of Knowing: The Development of Self, Voice, and Mind.* New York: Basic Books.

Bensimon, E.M. (1989). The meaning of "good" presidential leadership: A frame analysis. *Review of Higher Education* 12:107–23.

Bensimon, E.M. (1990a). The new president and understanding the campus as a culture. In W.G. Tierney (Ed.), *Assessing Academic Climates and Culture*, pp. 75–86. New Directions for Institutional Research, no. 68. San Francisco: Jossey-Bass.

Bensimon, E.M. (1990b). Viewing the presidency: Perceptual congruence between presidents and leaders on their campuses. *Leadership Quarterly* 1:71–90.

Bensimon, E.M. (1991a) [1989]. A feminist reinterpretation of presidents' definitions of leadership. *Peabody Journal of Education* 66(3):143–56.

Bensimon, E.M. (1991b). How college presidents use their administrative groups: "Real" and "illusory" teams. *Journal for Higher Education Management* 7:35–51.

Bensimon, E.M. (1991). The social processes through which faculty shape the image of a new president. *Journal of Higher Education* 62(6):637–60.

Bensimon, E.M., Neumann, A. & Birnbaum, R. (1989). *Making Sense of Administrative Leadership: The "L" Word in Higher Education.* Washington, D.C.: ASHE-ERIC Higher Education Reports.

Berger, P.L. & Luckmann, T. (1966). *The Social Construction of Reality.* Harmondsworth, Middlesex: Penguin.

Bernstein, A. (1991). Half full? Half empty? *Bulletin of the American Association for Higher Education* 43(9):8–9.

Birnbaum, R. (1988). *How Colleges Work: The Cybernetics of Academic Organization and Leadership*. San Francisco: Jossey-Bass.

Birnbaum, R. (1989). Responsibility without authority: The impossible job of the college president. In J. Smart (Ed.), *Higher Education Handbook of Theory and Research, vol. 5*. New York: Agathon.

Birnbaum, R. (in press). *How Academic Leadership Works: Understanding Success and Failure in the College Presidency*.

Blackmore, J. (1989). Educational leadership: A feminist critique and reconstruction. In J. Smyth (Ed.), *Critical Perspectives on Educational Leadership*, pp. 93–129. London: Falmer Press.

Bolman, L.G. & Deal, T.E. (1984). *Modern approaches to understanding and managing organizations*. San Francisco: Jossey-Bass.

Bolman, L.G. & Deal, T.E. (1991). *Reframing Organizations: Artistry, Choice, and Leadership*. San Francisco: Jossey-Bass.

Burrell, G. & Morgan, G. (1979). *Sociological Paradigms and Organisational Analysis*. London: Heinemann.

Chaffee, E.E. (1984). Successful strategic management in small private colleges. *Journal of Higher Education* 55:212–41.

Chaffee, E.E. & Tierney, W.G. (1988). *Collegiate Culture and Leadership Strategies*. New York: American Council on Education/Macmillan.

Citing sexism, Stanford doctor quits. (1991). *New York Times*, 4 June, p. A22.

Cleveland, H. (1985). *The Knowledge Executive: Leadership in an Information Society*. New York: Truman Talley.

Cohen, M. D. & March, J. G. (1974). *Leadership and Ambiguity: The American College Presidency*. New York: McGraw-Hill.

Cooper, R. & Burrell, G. (1988). Modernism, Postmodernism, and Organizational Analysis. *Organization Studies* 9(1):91–112.

Cox, A. (1989). Managing without hierarchy: Even "flat" companies need leaders. *New York Times*, 20 Aug.

Cox, A. (1991). Scrap consensus, try diversity. *New York Times*, 7 Apr., p. 11.

DePalma, A. (1991). Separate ethnic worlds grow on campus. *New York Times*, 18 May, p. 1.

Dyer, W.G. (1987). *Team Building: Issues and Alternatives*. Reading, Mass.: Addison-Wesley.

Eisenstat, R.A. & Cohen, S.G. (1990). Summary: Top management group. In J. Richard Hackman (Ed.) *Groups That Work (and Those That Don't): Creating Conditions for Effective Teamwork*. San Francisco: Jossey-Bass.

Fallows, J. (1989). *More Like Us*. Boston: Houghton Mifflin.

Ferguson, K. (1984). *The Feminist Case Against Bureaucracy*. Philadelphia: Temple University Press.

Freire, P. (1984). *Pedagogy of the Oppressed*. New York: Continuum.

Frost, P.J., Moore, L.F., Louis, M.R., Lundberg, C.C. & Martin, J. (Eds.). (1991). *Reframing Organizational Culture*. Newbury Park, Calif.: Sage.

Gabarro, J.J. (1987). *The Dynamics of Taking Charge*. Boston, Mass.: Harvard Business School Press.

Gardiner, J.J. (1988). Building leadership teams. In M. Green (Ed.), *Leaders for *a New Era*, pp. 137–53. New York: American Council on Education/Macmillan.

Gergen, K. (1991). *The Saturated Self*. New York: Basic Books.

Gilligan, C. (1982). *In a Different Voice: Psychological Theory and Women's Development*. Cambridge: Harvard University Press.

Gilligan, C., Lyons, N.P., & Hanmer, T.J. (Eds.). (1990). *Making Connections: The Relational Worlds of Adolescent Girls at Emma Willard School*. Cambridge, Mass.: Harvard University Press.

Gilmore, T.N. (1988). *Making a Leadership Change: How Organizations and Leaders Can Handle Leadership Transitions Successfully*. San Francisco: Jossey-Bass.

Gioia, D.A. (1986). Symbols, scripts, and sensemaking: Creating meaning in the organizational experience. In H.P. Sims, Jr. & D.A. Gioia (Eds.), *The Thinking Organization, Dynamics of Organizational Social Cognition*, pp. 49–74. San Francisco: Jossey-Bass.

Giroux, H.A. (1990). The politics of postmodernism: Rethinking the boundaries of race and ethnicity. *Journal of Urban and Cultural Studies* 1(1): 5–38.

Goleman, D. (1988). Recent studies help explain why some meetings fail and others succeed. *New York Times*, 7 June, p. C9.

Goodman, P. (1962). *The Community of Scholars*. New York: Random House.

Greene, M. (1988). *The Dialectic of Freedom*. New York: Teachers College Press.

Greenfield, T.B. (1980). The man who comes back through the door in the wall: Discovering truth, discovering self, discovering organization. *Educational Administration Quarterly* 16:26–59.

Greenfield, T.B. (1984). Leaders and schools: Willfulness and nonnatural order in organizations. In T.J. Sergiovanni and J.E. Corbally (Eds.), *Leadership and Organizational Culture*, pp. 142–69. Urbana: University of Illinois Press.

Guskin, A.E. & Bassis, M.A. (1985). Leadership styles and institutional renewal. In R.M. Davis (Ed.), *Leadership and Institutional Renewal. New Directions for Higher Education*. San Francisco: Jossey-Bass.

Harding, S. (1983). Why has the sex-gender system become visible only now? In S. Harding & M. Hintikka (Eds.), *Discovering Reality: Feminist Perspectives on Epistemology, Methodology and Philosophy of Science*. Dordrecht, Netherlands: Reidel.

Janis, I.L. (1972). *Victims of Groupthink*. Boston: Houghton-Mifflin.

Kanter, R.M. (1977). *Men and Women of the Corporation*. New York: Basic Books.

Kanter, R.M. (1983). *The Change Masters*. New York: Simon & Schuster.

Maher, F. (1985). Pedagogies for the gender-balanced classroom. *Journal of Thought* 20:48–64.

McDade, S. (1987). *Higher Education Leadership: Enhancing Skills through Professional Development Programs*. Washington, D.C.: ASHE-ERIC Higher Education Reports.

Meyerson, D. & Martin, J. (1987). Cultural change: An integration of three different views. *Journal of Management Studies* 24:623–47.

Miles, M.C. & Huberman, A.M. (1984). *Qualitative Data Analysis: A Source-book of New Methods*. Newbury Park, Calif.: Sage.

Millett, J. D. (1962). *An Essay on Organization: The Academic Community*. New York: McGraw-Hill.

Morgan, G. (1986). *Images of Organization*. Newbury Park, Calif.: Sage.

Morgan, G. (1988). *Riding the Waves of Change: Developing Managerial Competencies for a Turbulent World*. San Francisco: Jossey-Bass.

Neumann, A. (1989). Strategic leadership: The changing orientations of college presidents. *Review of Higher Education* 12:137–51.

Neumann, A. (1990a). Making mistakes: Error and learning in the college presidency. *Journal of Higher Education* 4:386–407.

Neumann, A. (1990b). On the making of 'good times' and 'hard times': The social construction of resource stress. Paper presented at the meeting of the Association for the Study of Higher Education, Portland, Oreg. (November).

Neumann, A. (1991a). Context, cognition, and culture: A case analysis of collegiate leadership and cultural change. Paper presented at the meeting of the American Educational Research Association, Chicago, Ill. (April).

Neumann, A. (1991b). Defining 'good faculty leadership.' *Thought and Action* [Journal of the National Education Association] 7:45–60.

Neumann, A. (1991c). The thinking team: Toward a cognitive model of administrative teamwork in higher education. *Journal of Higher Education* 62:485–513.

Neumann, A. (in press a). College planning: A cultural perspective. *Journal for Higher Education Management*.

Neumann, A. (in press b). Colleges under pressure: Budgeting, presidential competence, and faculty uncertainty. *Leadership Quarterly*.

Neumann, A. (1992). Double vision: The experience of institutional stability. *Review of Higher Education* 15(4):341–71.

Neumann, A. & Bensimon, E.M. (1990). Constructing the presidency: College presidents' images of their leadership roles, a comparative study. *Journal of Higher Education* 61(6):678–701.

Noddings, N. (1984). *Caring: A Feminine Approach to Ethics & Moral Education*. Berkeley: University of California Press.

Norman, M. (1988). Lessons: A university run by women teaches through the way it is managed. *New York Times*, 18 May.

Parker, G.M. (1990). *Team Players and Teamwork*. San Francisco: Jossey-Bass.

Pettigrew, A.W. (1979). On studying organizational cultures. *Administrative Science Quarterly* 24:570–81.

Reich, R. (1987). Entrepreneurship reconsidered: The team as hero. *Harvard Business Review* 65(3):77–83.

Rice, R.E. & Austin, A.E. (1988). High faculty morale: What exemplary colleges do right. *Change* 20:51–8.

Rogers, C.R. & Roethlisberger, F.J. (1952). Barriers and gateways to communication. *Harvard Business Review* 30 (4):28–34.

Rosaldo, R. (1989). *Culture and Truth: The Remaking of Social Analysis*. Boston: Beacon Press.

Schein, E.H. (1987). *Process Consultation. Vol. 2. Lessons from Managers and Consultants.* Reading, Mass. Addison-Wesley.

Schon, D.A. (1983). *The Reflective Practitioner.* New York: Basic Books.

Schutz, A. (1967). *The Phenomenology of the Social World,* trans. G. Walsh & F. Lehnert. Evanston, Ill.: Northwestern University Press. (Originally published 1932).

Smircich, L. (1983). Concepts of culture and organizational analysis. *Administrative Science Quarterly* 28:339–58.

Smircich, L. & Morgan, G. (1982). Leadership: The management of meaning. *Journal of Applied Behavioral Science* 18(3):257–73.

Smyth, J. (Ed.). (1989). *Critical Perspectives on Educational Leadership.* London: Falmer Press.

Tannen, D. (1990). *You Just Don't Understand: Women and Men in Conversation.* New York: William Morrow.

Tierney, W.G. (1988). *The Web of Leadership: The Presidency in Higher Education.* Greenwich, Conn.: JAI Press.

Tierney, W.G. (in press). *Building Communities of Difference: Higher Education in the 21st Century.* Granby, Mass.: Bergin & Garvey.

Walker, D.E. (1979). *The Effective Administrator.* San Francisco: Jossey-Bass.

Weick, K.E. (1979). *The Social Psychology of Organizing,* 2d ed. Reading, Mass.: Addison-Wesley.

Weick, K.E. (1983). Contradictions in a community of scholars: The cohesion-accuracy tradeoff. *Review of Higher Education* 6(4):253–67.

White, J.W. (1986). Putting together a winning presidential team. *Association of Governing Boards (AGB) Reports* 28(4):29–31.

Zaleznick, A. (1989). *The Managerial Mystique: Restoring Leadership in Business.* New York: Harper & Row.

Zuboff, S. (1988). *In the Age of the Smart Machine.* New York: Basic Books.

Index